One Day At A Time

A Daily Devotional Guide For

Each Day Of The Year

Rev. Allen Smith, M.R.Ed., D.D., Th.D.

ISBN: **1492305960**
ISBN-13: **978-1492305965**

*All Scripture quotations are taken from the King James Version
of the Holy Bible.*

Published by
Lighthouse International Ministries
http://sgospe7.wix.com/allensmithbooks
https://www.facebook.com/allensmithbooks
https://twitter.com/revallensmith

DEDICATION

This book is dedicated to both of my daughters,
Tammy Reed and Suzy Copeland.

CONTENTS

ACKNOWLEDGMENTS

I am thankful for the guidance of the
Jimmy Swaggart Expositor's Study Bible
during the compiling of this daily devotional.

If you are interested in obtaining your own copy of the Expositor's Study Bible,
please go to: www.jsm.org
Or
http://www.amazon.com/The-Expositors-Study-Bible-ebook/dp/B006P58FIS

CHAPTER 1 - JANUARY

JANUARY 1

1 John 4:9 (KJV) In this was manifested the love of God toward us, because that God sent his only begotten Son into the world, that we might live through him.

What a thought! God actually loves us so much, that He sent His only begotten Son to this earth. He did it for the express purpose of providing a way for us to have communion with Him. It is only through Jesus Christ and what He did at Calvary that we can have true life. It is because we live through Him, as He lives through us.

(Read Galatians 2:20)

*****

JANUARY 2

1 Peter 1:18-19 (KJV) (18) Forasmuch as ye know that ye were not redeemed with corruptible things, *as* silver and gold, from your vain conversation *received* by tradition from your fathers; (19) But with the precious blood of Christ, as of a lamb without blemish and without spot:

It took something special to redeem you back to God. Your redemption could not be purchased with silver, gold, or any other precious substance. It took the ***blood*** of Jesus! The lifestyle that you live because of religious traditions cannot redeem you! It takes the ***blood*** of Jesus! Jesus is the one and only Lamb of God! He is the one and only sacrifice for sin!

(Read Acts 20:28)

*****

JANUARY 3

Titus 3:5 (KJV) Not by works of righteousness which we have done, but according to his mercy he saved us, by the washing of regeneration, and renewing of the Holy Ghost;

It is absolutely impossible for man to perform works of righteousness in order to be saved. It is only because and through the ***blood*** shed on the cross of Calvary that we can receive salvation. The ***blood*** of Jesus washes away our sin and regenerates us. It is actually the Holy Ghost who carries out the work of regeneration, but only through the ***blood*** of Jesus. This is done when we exhibit faith in Jesus Christ and what He did at Calvary.

(Read 1 John 1:7)

JANUARY 4

2 Peter 1:4 (KJV) Whereby are given unto us exceeding great and precious promises: that by these ye might be partakers of the divine nature, having escaped the corruption that is in the world through lust.

Oh, the promises of God! Those precious promises found in the Bible hold the answers to all of life's problems. The very first promise is that He will implant His nature in you. This comes to everyone at the time they are born again. This verse describes the salvation experience of the sinner, and the sanctification of the saint.

(Read John 1:12)

*****

JANUARY 5

Acts 13:39 (KJV) And by him all that believe are justified from all things, from which ye could not be justified by the law of Moses.

By and through Jesus and His sacrifice on the cross, we are justified! This declares that we are absolved, or declared free from *all* blame. It does not mean some things, it means *ALL* things. The Law of Moses could not do that. It took the *blood* of Jesus, and faith in what Jesus did on Calvary.

(Read Romans 3:28)

*****

JANUARY 6

John 15:5 (KJV) I am the vine, ye *are* the branches: He that abideth in me, and I in him, the same bringeth forth much fruit: for without me ye can do nothing.

Jesus is the vine, the **true** vine! The vine is not the church. It is not a particular preacher, or even a particular doctrine. It is Jesus and Jesus alone. Believers in Jesus are the branches. Everything we receive from God comes to us through Jesus and His sacrifice on the cross. When we realize this and practice it, then the Holy Ghost can and will develop fruit within our lives. Without His sacrifice on Calvary, we cannot do anything.

(Read Philippians 1:11)

*****

JANUARY 7

Romans 8:17 (KJV) And if children, then heirs; heirs of God, and joint-heirs with Christ; if so be that we suffer with *him*, that we may be also glorified together.

Wow! Children of God! As children of God, we are heirs of God. But, it does not stop there. We are also joint heirs with Jesus Christ! That means everything that belongs to Jesus also belongs to us, because of His sacrifice on Calvary. As He suffered for us on the cross, we suffered with Him. He took our place on the cross. He has been glorified, and we too shall be glorified one day, and it was all made possible because of Calvary.

(Read 1 John 3:2)

*****

JANUARY 8

Colossians 2:9-10 (KJV) (9) For in him dwelleth all the fulness of the Godhead bodily. (10) And ye are complete in him, which is the head of all principality and power:

In Jesus Christ dwells all the fullness of the Godhead bodily. This is speaking of the Godhead as to essence. Jesus is the completion and He is the fullness of the Godhead. The believer is complete in Him. We are complete in Him because of His sacrifice at Calvary. He is not head over just the church, but He is also over all those who oppose Him.

(Read Philippians 2:10-11)

*****

JANUARY 9

1 John 2:1 (KJV) My little children, these things write I unto you, that ye sin not. And if any man sin, we have an advocate with the Father, Jesus Christ the righteous:

Contrary to popular belief, the Lord saves us from sin, not in sin. As believers in Jesus, we do not have to sin. We receive victory over sin because of the sacrifice Jesus made on the cross. But, if we do sin, we can and should go back to the foot of the cross and ask forgiveness for that sin. Jesus has promised to make intercession for us.

(Read Hebrews 7:25–26)

*****

JANUARY 10

1 Timothy 1:1 (KJV) Paul, an apostle of Jesus Christ by the commandment of God our Saviour, and Lord Jesus Christ, *which is* our hope;

The message given to the Apostle Paul was the message of **grace**. This message was given to him by the Holy Ghost. Jesus is our hope because of what He did at Calvary.

(Read Colossians 1:27)

*****

JANUARY 11

Colossians 3:4 (KJV) When Christ, *who is* our life, shall appear, then shall ye also appear with him in glory.

As Paul writes to the Colossian church here, he is referring to the rapture of the church. At that time, every saint will be given a glorified body. What a time that will be, as we meet Jesus in the air!

(Read 1 Corinthians 15:51–57)

*****

JANUARY 12

Ephesians 2:13-14 (KJV) (13) But now in Christ Jesus ye who sometimes were far off are made nigh by the blood of Christ. (14) For he is our peace, who hath made both one, and hath broken down the middle wall of partition *between us*;

Jesus Christ is the basis of our salvation. There was a time when we were far from the Lord, but through His blood that changed. Just think about it, the death of Jesus Christ on the cross changed the relationship of God with mankind. Through His sacrificial atoning death, Jesus reconciled an entire world to Himself. Because of what He did, we have total peace with God. We are no longer two races (Jew and Gentile), but one race. There is no longer a wall between us. If we are all saved, then we are all Christians.

(Read John 10:16)

*****

JANUARY 13

Jeremiah 23:6 (KJV) In his days Judah shall be saved, and Israel shall dwell safely: and this *is* his name whereby he shall be called, THE LORD OUR RIGHTEOUSNESS.

In this verse, Jeremiah is referring to the days of the Messiah. Specifically, he is talking about the 1,000 year reign of Jesus Christ upon the earth. This is sometimes referred to as the "Millennial Reign". At that time, Judah will be saved, where at the present time, they are lost.

(Read Romans 9:5)

*****

JANUARY 14

1 Corinthians 6:19 (KJV) What? know ye not that your body is the temple of the Holy Ghost *which is* in you, which ye have of God, and ye are not your own?

Did you know that your body is the Temple of the Holy Ghost? That is right, if you are saved, then He is living in you.

You are actually His sanctuary. Since your body now belongs to God, it should be treated properly. You are not your own, you belong to the Lord.

(Read 1 Corinthians 3:16-17)

*****

JANUARY 15

2 Thessalonians 2:13 (KJV) But we are bound to give thanks alway to God for you, brethren beloved of the Lord, because God hath from the beginning chosen you to salvation through sanctification of the Spirit and belief of the truth:

Do you understand this? God has chosen you! Because you repented of your sins, and called out to Him to save you, He has chosen you. We are saved by trusting in Jesus and His sacrifice on the cross. We are sanctified by continuing to trust in what He did. It does no good to trust in man, or even the church. It takes trusting in Jesus and His work on the cross.

(Read 1 Peter 1:2)

*****

JANUARY 16

Ephesians 3:16 (KJV) That he would grant you, according to the riches of his glory, to be strengthened with might by his Spirit in the inner man;

What a promise! The "He" here is referring to Jesus Christ. He has promised to strengthen you. But, what will He use in order to do that? In this verse, Paul is referring to the revealed perfections of God, not just His grace and power.

Provided that our faith is on Jesus Christ and what He did on Calvary, He will do it through the works of the Holy Ghost.

(Read Ephesians 1:19-20)

*****

JANUARY 17

Romans 8:15 (KJV) For ye have not received the spirit of bondage again to fear; but ye have received the Spirit of adoption, whereby we cry, Abba, Father.

When we were saved, the shackles of bondage were broken off of us. However, if we try to live after a system of works and laws, we will place ourselves back under bondage. This type of living creates a perpetual climate of fear in our lives. We have been adopted by the Holy Ghost. We are now a part of the family of God. Because of this, we can now call God "Father". This is all because of the sacrifice of Jesus Christ.

(Read John 1:12)

*****

JANUARY 18

John 15:26 (KJV) But when the Comforter is come, whom I will send unto you from the Father, *even* the Spirit of truth, which proceedeth from the Father, he shall testify of me:

The Comforter is the Holy Ghost, who is our helper. Jesus is the one who baptizes with the Holy Ghost. The Holy Ghost is the "Spirit of Truth", and He moved on men of old, starting with Moses, to write the Word of God that we now have. The Father sent the Holy Ghost in the name and authority of Jesus Christ. Even today, He is still testifying about what Jesus did on the cross of Calvary.

(Read Matthew 3:11-12)

JANUARY 19

Ephesians 4:30 (KJV) And grieve not the holy Spirit of God, whereby ye are sealed unto the day of redemption.

Did you know that the utterance of evil and worthless words is repulsive to the Holy Ghost? Did you know that you can cause the Holy Ghost to be grieved? The Holy Ghost is the seal that God has placed on us. We should do everything we can to please Him.

(Read Ephesians 1:13)

*****

JANUARY 20

John 16:13 (KJV) Howbeit when he, the Spirit of truth, is come, he will guide you into all truth: for he shall not speak of himself; but whatsoever he shall hear, *that* shall he speak: and he will show you things to come.

The Spirit of Truth which is the Holy Ghost was given on the day of Pentecost. If we keep our faith in Jesus and His sacrifice, then the Holy Ghost can show us the truth. He doesn't bring some truth, but "all truth". He does not testify about Himself, but rather about Jesus and His sacrifice. The things to come is referring to the promises of the New Covenant.

(Read John 14:26)

*****

JANUARY 21

Ephesians 2:19 (KJV) Now therefore ye are no more strangers and foreigners, but fellow-citizens with the saints, and of the household of God;

We were once strangers from God, for we did not know Him. However, since we received salvation, we are no longer strangers from Him. We are now in fellowship with Him. We now have a progressive relationship with God. This means we should be growing closer to Him each day.

(Read Ephesians 2:12-13

*****

JANUARY 22

Galatians 2:20 (KJV) I am crucified with Christ: nevertheless I live; yet not I, but Christ liveth in me: and the life which I now live in the flesh I live by the faith of the Son of God, who loved me, and gave himself for me.

This is the foundation of our victory, the crucifixion of Jesus Christ. We now are living a new life! The old man has passed away, we are a brand new creature. We do not live this life in our own strength and ability, but in the strength of the Holy Ghost. Christ lives in us and we live in Him. We must always keep our faith in Jesus Christ and what He did at Calvary.

(Read Romans 6:3-5)

*****

JANUARY 23

Romans 12:1 (KJV) I beseech you therefore, brethren, by the mercies of God, that ye present your bodies a living sacrifice, holy, acceptable unto God, *which is* your reasonable service.

Paul is begging us to listen to what he has to say. All the promises we have been given, have nothing to do with what we have done, or what we deserve. It is all because of the mercy of God. The words "living sacrifice" used here is referring to the sacrifice of Jesus Christ. The only way we can offer this "living sacrifice", is to keep our faith in Jesus and His sacrifice on Calvary. This then gives the Holy Ghost the ability to work in our lives. This makes our bodies, the temple of God, holy and acceptable to God. In fact, that is all that God will accept. This is our reasonable service. If we try any other way, it will not be acceptable to God.

(Read 1 Corinthians 6:20)

*****

JANUARY 24

Jude 1:21 (KJV) Keep yourselves in the love of God, looking for the mercy of our Lord Jesus Christ unto eternal life.

We are to stay within God's love. This can only be done by continuing to have faith in Jesus Christ and His sacrifice on Calvary. This iş what first got us saved, and it will keep us sanctified in Him. In addition we should keep watching for the rapture of the church to take place.

(Read Titus 2:13)

*****

JANUARY 25

Romans 8:1 (KJV) *There is* **therefore now no condemnation to them which are in Christ Jesus, who walk not after the flesh, but after the Spirit.**

We no longer need to feel guilty because we have been baptized into His death. This is speaking of salvation through the shed **blood** at Calvary. We must remember that we are not to walk in the flesh, but in the Spirit. This simply means that we live by faith in Calvary. We do not try to serve Him through works of the flesh, which is referring to our own efforts. Our faith in the finished work of Calvary guarantees the help of the Holy Ghost. Through Him, we are guaranteed victory!

(Read Romans 6:3–5)

*****

JANUARY 26

Hebrews 2:14 (KJV) Forasmuch then as the children are partakers of flesh and blood, he also himself likewise took part of the same; that through death he might destroy him that had the power of death, that is, the devil;

We are reminded that we are human, not angelic in nature. Jesus Himself left Heaven and took upon Himself this same nature, He became man. He went to the death of the cross to defeat Satan. Jesus atoned for all sin, and in doing such He removed the cause of spiritual death for all who will believe in what He did.

(Read Hebrews 4:15-16)

*****

JANUARY 27

Psalms 130:7-8 (KJV) (7) Let Israel hope in the LORD: for with the LORD *there is* mercy, and with him *is* plenteous redemption. (8) And he shall redeem Israel from all his iniquities. Let us continue to keep our hope in the Lord, and what He has done for us.

This is a song of trust in God. It is a reminder to Israel and the Church of the abundant hope we have, as long as we take advantage of God's great plan of salvation.

(Read 1 Peter 2:24-25)

*****

JANUARY 28

Psalms 18:48 (KJV) He delivereth me from mine enemies: yea, thou liftest me up above those that rise up against me: thou hast delivered me from the violent man.

God always provided a way to deliver David from his enemies. In the same way, God through Jesus Christ has delivered us from our enemies, both physical and spiritual.

(Read Psalm 42:5)

*****

JANUARY 29

1 Peter 2:10 (KJV) Which in time past *were* not a people, but *are* now the people of God: which had not obtained mercy, but now have obtained mercy.

Without God, we simply do not have any standing. But now, because of what Jesus did at Calvary, we are children of God, if we have repented. He has provided us with His mercy, which is a product of His sacrifice on the cross.

(Read Romans 9:25-26)

*****

JANUARY 30

1 Peter 1:5 (KJV) Who are kept by the power of God through faith unto salvation ready to be revealed in the last time.

As our faith continues in Jesus and Calvary, the Holy Ghost applies His power on our behalf. He wants to make us ready for the rapture as we see the last days rapidly approaching.

Read John 10:28)

*****

JANUARY 31

Hebrews 11:16 (KJV) But now they desire a better *country*, that is, an heavenly: wherefore God is not ashamed to be called their God: for he hath prepared for them a city.

What a thought! Since being saved, we now seek something better than this old world. Like Abraham, we seek that Heavenly city that is not made by human hands. Because of our faith in Jesus and the blood that was shed for us, He has already prepared that city for us.

(Read Matthew 25:34).

FEBRUARY 1

Luke 10:25-27 (KJV) (25) And, behold, a certain lawyer stood up, and tempted him, saying, Master, what shall I do to inherit eternal life? (26) He said unto him, What is written in the law? how readest thou? (27) And he answering said, Thou shalt love the Lord thy God with all thy heart, and with all thy soul, and with all thy strength, and with all thy mind; and thy neighbour as thyself.

This lawyer was known to be an expert in the Mosaic Law. He was there to test the Lord's knowledge of the Law. It was unknown to him that Jesus was actually the Law. He wanted to know what he could do to inherit eternal life. He could not have asked a better question, for everyone is interested in its answer. Jesus did not waste any time in pointing this man directly to the Bible, the only authority. Jesus not only knew the word, but He understood it also. His answer was something we need to pay close attention to. Love the Lord with your whole heart. Love the Lord with your entire soul. Love the Lord with all of your mind. Love your neighbor as yourself. This should be our goal each and every day.

(Read Matthew 22:35–40)

*****

FEBRUARY 2

Luke 17:15 (KJV) And one of them, when he saw that he was healed, turned back, and with a loud voice glorified God,

Ten men were healed in this potion of Scripture. Out of the ten, only one of them returned to the Lord to thank Him. We should remember to thank and praise the Lord when He does something special for us. But, it should not stop there. We should be doing it on a continual basis.

(Read Matthew 15:31)

*****

FEBRUARY 3

Romans 6:17-18 (KJV) (17) But God be thanked, that ye were the servants of sin, but ye have obeyed from the heart that form of doctrine which was delivered you. (18) Being then made free from sin, ye became the servants of righteousness.

We were once slaves to the sin nature. That was before we were saved. But, when we heard about Jesus and Him being crucified, we became children of God. This doctrine of being saved by the **blood** was first given to the Apostle Paul, who then gave it to us through the Epistles he wrote. Jesus set us free from the sin nature. As long as we continue to have faith in what was done at Calvary, the sin nature no longer has power over us. Because of that faith, we are now slaves to righteousness, and are constantly pulled toward it.

(Read 1 Peter 4:2)

*****

FEBRUARY 4

Hebrews 12:9 (KJV) Furthermore we have had fathers of our flesh which corrected *us*, and we gave *them* reverence: shall we not much rather be in subjection unto the Father of spirits, and live?

Do we give God as much reverence as we do our earthly parents? We should be doing this, and much more. We need to remember that He is our eternal Heavenly Father, and He deserves so much more than we give Him.

(Read 2 Peter 1:4)

*****

FEBRUARY 5

1 John 5:1 (KJV) Whosoever believeth that Jesus is the Christ is born of God: and every one that loveth him that begat loveth him also that is begotten of him.

The word "believeth" is referring to our heart accepting that Jesus Christ died in our place on Calvary's cruel cross. He did it because He loves us. We are also reminded that we should love all of God's children.

(Read John 1:12)

FEBRUARY 6

Matthew 10:37 (KJV) He that loveth father or mother more than me is not worthy of me: and he that loveth son or daughter more than me is not worthy of me.

Jesus must come first in our lives, in all things that we do. If we have anything or anyone else in our lives, in a place greater than God is, then we are not worthy of Him. Let us take time right now to make sure that God has His proper place in our hearts and lives.

(Read Matthew 16:24)

*****

FEBRUARY 7

Luke 9:23 (KJV) And he said to *them* all, If an *man* will come after me, let him deny himself, and take up his cross daily, and follow me.

Here we find out what it takes to be a disciple. What did Jesus mean when He said "deny oneself"? He was talking about denying our own willpower, our self-will, and our own strength and ability. We need to depend totally on Jesus Christ. We need to lean toward and have faith in what Jesus accomplished on the cross. We must strive to do this on a daily basis, for our enemy, the devil, is constantly trying to move us away from the cross. He knows when we stop having faith in what Jesus did on the cross, that he can and will be able to defeat us. Look ever toward the victory provided at Calvary!

(Read 1 Corinthians 1:17–18)

*****

FEBRUARY 8

1 John 4:15 (KJV) Whosoever shall confess that Jesus is the Son of God, God dwelleth in him, and he in God.

John is talking about a lifetime confession here. He is talking about a change of heart, which brings about a change in the way we live. When this change is made within our heart and life, then and only then is there a joining together of ourselves with God. This union can only come about because of what Jesus did at the cross.

(Read 1 John 4:9)

*****

FEBRUARY 9

Romans 14:8 (KJV) For whether we live, we live unto the Lord; and whether we die, we die unto the Lord: whether we live therefore, or die, we are the Lord's.

Let us not forget, that everything we do in our lives is to be done as "unto the Lord". As a Christian, as long as we live, we are the Lord's. In addition, when we die, we are the Lord's. It should be our total desire for the Lord to be in complete control of our lives and our death.

(Read 2 Corinthians 5:15)

*****

FEBRUARY 10

John 13:15 (KJV) For I have given you an example, that ye should do as I have done to you.

Jesus gave us an example. He showed us that an individual can live for God. As long as we live by faith in the finished work of Calvary, God will give us the strength to live for Him.

(Read Matthew 11:29)

*****

FEBRUARY 11

1 Peter 2:6-7 (KJV) (6) Wherefore also it is contained in the scripture, Behold, I lay in Sion a chief corner stone, elect, precious: and he that believeth on him shall not be confounded. (7) Unto you therefore which believe *he is* precious: but unto them which be disobedient, the stone which the builders disallowed, the same is made the head of the corner,

Jesus Christ is our Chief Cornerstone. The Word declares if we believe, or put our faith in Him, we shall not be confounded or put to shame. The world may not want anything to do with Him, but we know that He provided the victory for us, through Calvary. One day, the world itself will have to answer to Him.

(Read Romans 9:33)

*****

FEBRUARY 12

Romans 8:9 (KJV) But ye are not in the flesh, but in the Spirit, if so be that the Spirit of God dwell in you. Now if any man have not the Spirit of Christ, he is none of his.

Paul is asking a question here. We can ask ourselves the same question. Since you are now a Christian and do not need to depend on the flesh any longer, why do you keep relying on the flesh? We now have the privilege of being led and enabled by the Holy Ghost. This is proved to us because of the finished work of Calvary. If we are truly saved, then we will be led by the Spirit.

(Read 1 Corinthians 2:11)

*****

FEBRUARY 13

Romans 8:14 (KJV) For as many as are led by the Spirit of God, they are the sons of God.

Are you being led by the Spirit? The Spirit will always point us back to Jesus, Calvary, and the resurrection. If so, we should have total victory in every part of our lives.

(Read 1 Corinthians 2:12)

*****

FEBRUARY 14

Psalms 38:3-4 (KJV) (3) *There is* **no soundness in my flesh because of thine anger; neither** *is there any* **rest in my bones because of my sin. (4) For mine iniquities are gone over mine head: as an heavy burden they are too heavy for me.**

It is hard to understand all Jesus has done for us. Jesus actually took our sins unto Himself. Because of this, He faced the wrath of God as He hung on the cross. The burden He carried was heavy, because He took the sins of the entire world on Himself. O, what a Saviour!

(Read Matthew 11:28-30)

*****

FEBRUARY 15

2 Corinthians 7:10 (KJV) For godly sorrow worketh repentance to salvation not to be repented of: but the sorrow of the world worketh death.

When we are faced with the convicting power of the Holy Ghost, we begin to see ourselves as God sees us. Then we begin to have Godly sorrow. This means our hearts desire is to be what God wants us to be. Repentance then takes place, and that is something we will never regret. The sorrow brought about by the world brings doubt, despair, and even depression.

(Read Acts 11:18)

*****

FEBRUARY 16

1 John 3:9 (KJV) Whosoever is born of God doth not commit sin; for his seed remaineth in him: and he cannot sin, because he is born of God.

As a child of God, we do not practice sin. This is because the Word of God is within us. As such, we cannot practice sin because the Spirit of God is there to let us know not to proceed if we start to do something we should not do. The heart of the true Christian cannot stand sin. If we continue a life of sin, then we cannot remain a child of God.

(Read 1 John 5:18)

*****

FEBRUARY 17

Galatians 5:24 (KJV) And they that are Christ's have crucified the flesh with the affections and lusts.

This is something that we cannot do in our own strength. This can only be done when we understand it was carried out by Jesus at the cross. We realize that we are baptize with Him in His death. This is the only thing that will bring out the proper results.

(Read Romans 6:3–5)

*****

FEBRUARY 18

Philippians 3:8 (KJV) Yea doubtless, and I count all things _but_ loss for the excellency of the knowledge of Christ Jesus my Lord: for whom I have suffered the loss of all things, and do count them _but_ dung, that I may win Christ,

Paul cared to know nothing but Jesus and Him crucified. The more we study God's Word, and the more we pray to Him, the more we learn about Him. We should desire to have the same intimate companionship and communion with God that Paul had. Remember, next to Jesus Christ, everything else is nothing.

(Read 2 Peter 1:3)

*****

FEBRUARY 19

1 John 5:4 (KJV) For whatsoever is born of God overcometh the world: and this is the victory that overcometh the world, _even_ our faith.

If we obey God's Word, then we will be overcomers. If we do not, then we will live a life of defeat. It takes faith in Christ and His work on Calvary. Then and only then does the Holy Ghost have the liberty to work within our lives.

(Read Romans 8:1-2)

*****

FEBRUARY 20

1 John 2:15 (KJV) Love not the world, neither the things *that are* in the world. If any man love the world, the love of the Father is not in him.

Loving the world has to do with loving and taking part in that system wherein Satan is the head. Our Heavenly Father will not share His love that comes only from Him, with the world. You are His child, and He cares for you.

(Read James 4:4)

*****

FEBRUARY 21

Romans 8:5 (KJV) For they that are after the flesh do mind the things of the flesh; but they that are after the Spirit the things of the Spirit.

Those that are after the flesh, are trying to live for God by some other means than having faith in the sacrifice of Jesus on the cross. By placing our faith in Jesus and His sacrifice, and doing it exclusively, you are doing what the Spirit of God desires. This is the only way to receive and keep victory.

(Read *Galatians 5:24-25*)

*****

FEBRUARY 22

Philippians 3:20 (KJV) For our conversation is in heaven; from whence also we look for the Saviour, the Lord Jesus Christ:

The word "conversation" used here is referring to "citizenship". So, if we have our citizenship in Heaven, it means we are looking for the Lord Jesus Christ to come. Jesus is the only way. There is no other way to Heaven.

(Read Philippians 1:27)

*****

FEBRUARY 23

2 Corinthians 5:14-15 (KJV) (14) For the love of Christ constraineth us; because we thus judge, that if one died for all, then were all dead: (15) And *that* he died for all, that they which live should not henceforth live unto themselves, but unto him which died for them, and rose again.

What Jesus did for us on Calvary shows us His love toward us. He died for the whole world, for all time. When He did this, we were all dead in our trespasses and sins. But, He died for all! This was the supreme sacrifice. Our ransom was paid for by His blood. Once we have accepted Jesus, then we belong to Him. It is now up to us to do His will in our lives.

(Read Romans 14:7-8)

*****

FEBRUARY 24

1 John 4:6 (KJV) We are of God: he that knoweth God heareth us; he that is not of God heareth not us. Hereby know we the spirit of truth, and the spirit of error.

Do we follow the "Spirit of Truth"? That is the Holy Ghost. He leads into all truth. That truth is Jesus and Him crucified. The "spirit of error" is referring to any doctrine that ignores the sacrifice of Jesus on the cross. Those doctrines are espoused by Satan and carried out by his demonic forces.

(Read 1 Timothy 4:1)

*****

FEBRUARY 25

1 John 2:19 (KJV) They went out from us, but they were not of us; for if they had been of us, they would *no doubt* have continued with us: but *they went out*, that they might be made manifest that they were not all of us.

John is speaking about a group of people who claimed to be a part of the true church. But, John further states "they were not part of us". You see, they had fallen for false doctrines, and they left. In following after the false doctrines, they turned their backs on Jesus and His sacrifice. Let us be sure to continue in God's Word, and make sure we do not fall for false doctrines, and lose out with God.

(Read 2 Peter 1:12)

*****

FEBRUARY 26

Psalms 119:127-129 (KJV) (127) Therefore I love thy commandments above gold; yea, above fine gold. (128) Therefore I esteem all *thy* precepts *concerning* all *things to be* right; *and* I hate every false way. (129) Thy testimonies *are* wonderful: therefore doth my soul keep them.

Jesus loved the Word of God. He is the Word of God. We are told here of the inspiration of the Word. We are also told of its perfection, inerrancy, and its authority. Jesus' love for the Word of God and the grief that He feels because men ignore it is the emphasis of these verses. O, that we would develop a greater love for God's Word!

(Read Psalm 119:104)

*****

FEBRUARY 27

Luke 6:3 (KJV) And Jesus answering them said, Have ye not read so much as this, what David did, when himself was an hungered, and they which were with him;

Here we find "Religion" attacking Jesus. These men had come with the purpose of destroying Him. But Jesus referred them to the Word of God. The letter kills, but the Spirit brings life. Religion destroys, but Christianity is a relationship with Jesus Christ. How is your relationship?

(Read Mark 3:1–6)

*****

FEBRUARY 28

1 John 4:7 (KJV) Beloved, let us love one another: for love is of God; and every one that loveth is born of God, and knoweth God.

This verse is speaking of "Agape" love. That's the God kind of love. The world knows nothing about this kind of love, In fact, churches caught up in a religious system know nothing about this type of love either. The God kind of love cannot be faked! Something will always take place to show what type of love a person has. What type of love do you possess? Is it the God kind of love, or is it a religious or worldly love?

(Read 1 John 3:10-11)

*****

FEBRUARY 29

1 John 3:19-21 (KJV) (19) And hereby we know that we are of the truth, and shall assure our hearts before him. (20) For if our heart condemn us, God is greater than our heart, and knoweth all things. (21) Beloved, if our heart condemn us not, *then* have we confidence toward God.

If we have the Love of God, then that guarantees truth. Are we showing love the way we should be? If so, our heart will tell us! Our heart will let us know if something is wrong, providing we listen to it. God knows how bad we actually are, yet He still loves us. God knows our heart. Nothing is hidden from Him. Our heart knows if we have unconfessed sin in our lives. If we do, then it's time to go to God in prayer and ask

His forgiveness.

(Read Hebrews 10:22-2

CHAPTER 3 - MARCH

MARCH 1

Psalms 84:11 (KJV) For the LORD God *is* a sun and shield: the LORD will give grace and glory: no good *thing* will he withhold from them that walk uprightly.

Just thinking about these promises makes me want to shout! He is our light, to guide us on our journey, and He is our shield to protect us during that journey. He has also promised not to withhold any good thing from us. At Calvary, He provided the grace and glory to give us eternal life. But, we need to allow Him to give us those "good things" He desires to give us. It is His choice, not ours.

(Read Isaiah 60:19-20)

*****

MARCH 2

Psalms 73:26 (KJV) My flesh and my heart faileth: *but* **God** *is* **the strength of my heart, and my portion for ever.**

Leaning on our own strength always brings failure. We need to learn that God is our strength. Two thousand years ago at Calvary, Jesus provided the victory over everything the Devil can throw at us. Anything and everything we need can be provided by God, if only we will have faith in Him and what He has already done.

(Read Psalm 119:81)

*****

MARCH 3

Psalms 46:1-2 (KJV) (1) God *is* **our refuge and strength, a very present help in trouble. (2) Therefore will not we fear, though the earth be removed, and though the mountains be carried into the midst of the sea;**

God is our shelter and protection when the enemy comes against us. He is our strength, when our own strength has failed us. It does not matter what changes on this earth, or what the enemy throws against us, God is constant in our lives. He never changes. He will always do what He says He will do, if we continue to have faith in Jesus and His victory over death, Hell, and the grave.

(Read Psalm 4:1)

MARCH 4

Psalms 48:14 (KJV) For this God *is* our God for ever and ever: he will be our guide *even* unto death.

What a promise! He is our God, now and forever. He has provided a way for us to live for Him during this short lifespan we have here on earth. He has provided a way for us to enter into eternity with Him. He will guide us through this life, and into eternal life, if we will only allow Him to do it.

(Read Revelation 21:4)

*****

MARCH 5

Psalms 3:3 (KJV) But thou, O LORD, *art* a shield for me; my glory, and the lifter up of mine head.

Yes, God is our shield of protection. He is our glory, for we have no glory in ourselves. As God lifted David up, and placed him on the throne of Israel, He will lift us up also, and take care of us. We just need to keep Him first in our lives.

(Read Psalm 27:6)

*****

MARCH 6

1 Corinthians 3:21-23 (KJV) (21) Therefore let no man glory in men. For all things are yours; (22) Whether Paul, or Apollos, or Cephas, or the world, or life, or death, or things present, or things to come; all are yours; (23) And ye are Christ's; and Christ *is* God's.

We should not glory in man, for all glory belongs to God. Everything that God gives, is available to every believer, as long as it is in God's will. God does not play favorites, what He does for one, He will do for others. The Lord is ruler of all things, and nothing can happen to us unless He allows it.

(Read Galatians 3:29)

*****

MARCH 7

Ephesians 1:3 (KJV) Blessed *be* the God and Father of our Lord Jesus Christ, who hath blessed us with all spiritual blessings in heavenly *places* in Christ:

We should always bless God for everything He has done for us. Every benefit of the atonement has come from God through Jesus Christ. Every divine blessing is ours because of Jesus Christ and what He did at Calvary.

(Read 2 Corinthians 1:3-4)

*****

MARCH 8

Colossians 1:14 (KJV) In whom we have redemption through his blood, *even* **the forgiveness of sins:**

Redemption, what a wonderful word. It means deliverance upon payment of ransom. That's what Jesus did for us. He paid the ransom for us. That ransom was paid by His **blood**. At the cross, Jesus broke the power of sin. He took away its guilt. He set us free, through His **blood**.

(Read Romans 6:6)

*****

MARCH 9

Romans 3:24 (KJV) Being justified freely by his grace through the redemption that is in Christ Jesus:

Justified, another great word. It means to declare free from blame or sin. Through the blood Jesus shed on the cross, we are declared justified from our sins. What a wonderful thought. We cannot bring about our own justification, but when we repent of our sins, we are automatically justified in the eyes of God, because of Calvary.

(Read 2 Timothy 1:9)

*****

MARCH 10

Romans 5:10 (KJV) For if, when we were enemies, we were reconciled to God by the death of his Son, much more, being reconciled, we shall be saved by his life.

Another great word is reconciled. It means to reestablish a close relationship. Mankind once had a close relationship with God. The Bible tells us that Adam walked with God in the Garden of Eden. One day Adam sinned, and we all lost that fellowship with God. But, when Jesus died on the cross, He made a way to reestablish our relationship with God. All we have to do is repent. That means having a Godly sorrow for our sins. It means asking forgiveness for those sins. Finally, it means turning away from our wicked ways. When that all takes place, then the **blood** of Jesus reconciles us back to God.

(Read Colossians 1:20-21)

*****

MARCH 11

John 1:12 (KJV) But as many as received him, to them gave he power to become the sons of God, *even* to them that believe on his name:

Some have received Him in the past, and some continue to receive Him now. Here we are given one of the greatest promises in the Word of God. In accepting Him, it must be on His terms, and not ours. Jesus said He was the door. He is the only door. To believe on his name means to turn our lives over to Him completely. Having faith in Jesus and the sacrifice He made on Calvary.

(Read 1 John 3:1)

*****

MARCH 12

Matthew 11:28 (KJV) Come unto me, all *ye* that labour and are heavy laden, and I will give you rest.

In this verse, Jesus is revealing Himself to us as the one and only giver of salvation. He is reminding us that we don't earn salvation through works. It comes by accepting and having faith in Jesus Christ, and what He accomplished on the cross.

(Read Galatians 5:1)

*****

MARCH 13

John 10:28 (KJV) And I give unto them eternal life; and they shall never perish, neither shall any *man* pluck them out of my hand.

This is a promise no one else can match. He provides eternal life! Those that truly live their lives for God have nothing to fear. They do not need to fear eternal damnation. There is not a single outside force that can snatch us out of the hand of the Lord, but one can take one's self out of His hand. Let us make sure we stay in His hand.

(Read John 6:37)

*****

MARCH 14

Philippians 4:13 (KJV) I can do all things through Christ which strengtheneth me.

I can do all things. "All" means "all", and that is "all" that "all" means. We draw our strength from the Lord. He is the one who provides the victory. He provided that victory 2,000 years ago at Calvary.

(Read Colossians 1:11-13)

*****

MARCH 15

John 8:36 (KJV) If the Son therefore shall make you free, ye shall be free indeed.

Only Jesus can make us free. He accomplished that at Calvary. Once we place our faith in what He did at the cross, then we have that freedom. The world does not understand, nor can it give this freedom. It only comes through Jesus.

(Read Galatians 5:1)

MARCH 16

2 Thessalonians 2:16 (KJV) Now our Lord Jesus Christ himself, and God, even our Father, which hath loved us, and hath given *us* everlasting consolation and good hope through grace,

Jesus is our Lord, at least He should be. If he is our Lord, then our hearts desire is to please Him in everything we do. If we have the proper relationship with our Lord, then we can legally call God our Father. If we do not have a proper relationship with our Lord, then God is not our Father. This all comes to us because of Calvary.

(Read 1 Peter 1:3)

*****

MARCH 17

Romans 5:1(KJV) Therefore being justified by faith, we have peace with God through our Lord Jesus Christ:

The only way we can be justified is by faith. We cannot have faith in just anything, and expect to be justified. Faith in our parents will not make us justified. Faith in our church does not make us justified. Faith in our pastor does not make us justified. Only faith in Jesus Christ and His death on Calvary can justify us. We have the peace that the world does not understand because of the sacrifice of Jesus at Calvary.

(Read Romans 3:28)

MARCH 18

Ephesians 3:12 (KJV) In whom we have boldness and access with confidence by the faith of him.

"In whom" is referring to Jesus Christ. But, it does not stop there, for it also refers to what He did at Calvary. Because of the crucifixion, we can approach God with boldness. It actually provides us with access to God's throne room. Thank God for the atoning work of Jesus Christ.

(Read Hebrews 4:16)

*****

MARCH 19

1 Corinthians 15:57 (KJV) But thanks *be* to God, which giveth us the victory through our Lord Jesus Christ.

The victory was won 2,000 years ago at Calvary. It was won by and through the shed *blood* of Jesus. The resurrection formally approved what was done at Calvary. We have the victory through our Lord Jesus Christ.

(Read Romans 8:37)

*****

MARCH 20

1 Corinthians 3:16 (KJV) Know ye not that ye are the temple of God, and *that* the Spirit of God dwelleth in you?

Wow! We are the very Temple of God! This is where the Holy Ghost dwells. We are actually the permanent home of the Holy Ghost. What a thought.

(Read 2 Corinthians 6:16)

*****

MARCH 21

Romans 8:26 (KJV) Likewise the Spirit also helpeth our infirmities: for we know not what we should pray for as we ought: but the Spirit itself maketh intercession for us with groanings which cannot be uttered.

Infirmities could be speaking of sins, or diseases, or feebleness. It does not really matter which, Jesus sent the Holy Ghost to help us with all of these. We don't always know what or how to pray, but when this happens, the Holy Ghost will intercede for us. The groanings are not on the part of the Holy Ghost, but rather on our part. He will speak to God that which comes from our heart and what we are not able to put into words.

(Read Ephesians 6:18)

*****

MARCH 22

1 Peter 1:2 (KJV) Elect according to the foreknowledge of God the Father, through sanctification of the Spirit, unto obedience and sprinkling of the blood of Jesus Christ: Grace unto you, and peace, be multiplied.

Those who favorably decide to respond to the call of God through the Holy Ghost, are the elect of God. From the very beginning, God saw that a Saviour would be needed to redeem mankind. All who accept the Saviour are the elect. The Holy Ghost will sanctify us on the basis of the finished work of Calvary. This is where our faith must be. Both Grace and Peace come through the cross of Calvary. They will continue to multiply as long as we keep our faith in Jesus and what He did at Calvary.

(Read Hebrews 10:22-23)

*****

MARCH 23

Galatians 5:22-23 (KJV) (22) But the fruit of the Spirit is love, joy, peace, longsuffering, gentleness, goodness, faith, (23) Meekness, temperance: against such there is no law.

This is speaking of "one" fruit. As such, they should be looked at as a "whole", which means they grow equally. Because of these, Christians do not need a law. Let us remember, that this is the fruit of the Holy Ghost, and not of man. This fruit can only grow as we are being "lead by the Spirit". This can only happen as long as we continue to have faith in Jesus and His death on Calvary.

(Read Romans 6:6)

*****

MARCH 24

Acts 20:32 (KJV) And now, brethren, I commend you to God, and to the word of his grace, which is able to build you up, and to give you an inheritance among all them which are sanctified.

We have been placed in the capable hands of God, the one who is able to keep us. God uses the Word of Grace to keep us. This is the Gospel of Jesus Christ and Him crucified. It is the Word of God alone that is able to build us up. We are sanctified only by having faith in what Jesus did at Calvary. This gives the Holy Ghost the freedom to carry out His work in our lives. Remember, we cannot sanctify ourselves.

(Read Colossians 2:7-8)

*****

MARCH 25

Psalms 92:12-14 (KJV) (12) The righteous shall flourish like the palm tree: he shall grow like a cedar in Lebanon. (13) Those that be planted in the house of the LORD shall

flourish in the courts of our God. (14) They shall still bring forth fruit in old age; they shall be fat and flourishing;

The believer is here compared to a palm tree and to a cedar tree. The palm tree grows in sandy soil, and the cedar on a rugged mountain. One is nourished through a taproot, the other from above. One is beautiful, and the other is strong. We as Christians have a secret source of life. We receive our blessings from beneath, and from above. The Christian is morally beautiful and strong. We must remember that the wicked will flourish for a little while, but they will be cut off. But, those of us who are planted in God's Grace will prosper and bring forth fruit for eternity.

(Read Psalm 58:11)

*****

MARCH 26

Job 17:9 (KJV) The righteous also shall hold on his way, and he that hath clean hands shall be stronger and stronger.

Job spoke these words through faith. Job would not let anyone sway him from his hold on God. In fact, their accusations just made him stronger. It is up to us to learn from Job, and to be just as determined to serve God.

(Read Psalm 24:4-5)

*****

MARCH 27

1 John 5:14(KJV) And this is the confidence that we have in him, that, if we ask any thing according to his will, he heareth us:

If we have proper believing, then we will also have proper confidence, and proper assurance. We will know that if we ask anything within God's will, that He not only hears, He also answers. What a wonderful God we serve!

(Read 1 John 3:21-2

*****

MARCH 28

Psalms 27:5 (KJV) For in the time of trouble he shall hide me in his pavilion: in the secret of his tabernacle shall he hide me; he shall set me up upon a rock.

If we keep our faith in Christ and His sacrifice, when trouble comes, God will be with us. He has promised not to let any more to come on us than what we can bare. He has also promised to make a way of escape. He not only hides us from the enemy, but He also sets us on the Rock, which is Jesus.

(Read Psalm 32:7)

*****

MARCH 29

Romans 8:28 (KJV) And we know that all things work together for good to them that love God, to them who are the called according to *his* purpose.

Here is another great promise from the Word of God. But, we need to understand that conditions have been placed on it. The first condition is that it only applies to those who love God. The second says it is applied to those who are called according to His purpose. This means, that we are serving His purpose, and not our own. If both of these conditions are met, then all things will work together for our good.

(Read 2 Timothy 1:9)

*****

MARCH 30

Isaiah 26:3 (KJV) Thou wilt keep *him* in perfect peace, *whose* mind *is* stayed *on thee*: because he trusteth in thee.

True peace only comes from God. If we keep our mind firmly on Jesus and Him crucified, then He will give us perfect peace.

(Read John 14:27)

*****

MARCH 31

Psalms 37:37 (KJV) Mark the perfect *man*, and behold the upright: for the end of *that* man *is* peace.

There is only one perfect man, His name is Jesus. Our goal in life should be to be exactly what He wants us to be.

(Read Psalm 119:165).

CHAPTER 4 - APRIL

APRIL 1

Titus 3:8 (KJV) *This is* **a faithful saying, and these things I will that thou affirm constantly, that they which have believed in God might be careful to maintain good works. These things are good and profitable unto men.**

Titus says this is a trustworthy statement, something we can rely on. He is stating that the preacher and teacher of the Gospel should constantly preach Jesus and Him crucified. The greatest good work of all is to tell others what Jesus has done for them.

(Read 1 Timothy 6:18-19)

*****

APRIL 2

1 Corinthians 10:31(KJV) Whether therefore ye eat, or drink, or whatsoever ye do, do all to the glory of God.

Whatever we do, or where ever we go, we should have one question in mind. Does this bring glory to God?

(Read Colossians 3:17)

*****

APRIL 3

1 John 2:6 (KJV) He that saith he abideth in him ought himself also so to walk, even as he walked.

If we claim to be a child of God, then the life we live should show everyone that we are a child of God. Jesus set the example for us, and we should be following His example.

(Read John 15:4-5)

*****

APRIL 4

Hebrews 13:20-21 (KJV) (20) Now the God of peace, that brought again from the dead our Lord Jesus, that great shepherd of the sheep, through the blood of the

everlasting covenant, (21) Make you perfect in every good work to do his will, working in you that which is well-pleasing in his sight, through Jesus Christ; to whom *be* glory for ever and ever. Amen.

This proclaims that through the sacrifice of Jesus on the cross, God made peace between Him and fallen man. Jesus is that great shepherd, for it is He who died on Calvary in our place. Not only did He die on the cross, but He also resurrected from the grave, victorious over death, Hell, and the grave. Because of this, we have an everlasting covenant with God. The Holy Ghost was sent to work sanctification in our lives, to be constantly drawing us closer to God. Only through Jesus Christ can we do what is acceptable to God. This is because of what He did at Calvary.

(Read Philippians 2:13)

*****

APRIL 5

Colossians 3:17 (KJV) And whatsoever ye do in word or deed, *do* all in the name of the Lord Jesus, giving thanks to God and the Father by him.

Regardless of what we do, everything is to be done in the name of the Lord. In addition, we should never fail to praise and thank Him in all things.

(Read Ephesians 5:20)

*****

APRIL 6

Romans 13:11 (KJV) And that, knowing the time, that now *it is* high time to awake out of sleep: for now *is* our salvation nearer than when we believed.

If we know our Bible, then we know we are living in the last days. As such, we need to shake ourselves and wake up to the fact that we should be doing all we can to reach the lost. Truly, the rapture is much nearer than we think.

(Read Hebrews 10:25)

*****

APRIL 7

Luke 7:15 (KJV) And he that was dead sat up, and began to speak. And he delivered him to his mother.

Can you imagine what this must have been like? Oh, the joy that must have possessed this family. How happy this mother must have been. One day, we will take our place in heaven. When we do, our family that has gone on before us will be just as excited!

(Read Acts 20:27)

*****

APRIL 8

Ecclesiastes 9:10 (KJV) Whatsoever thy hand findeth to do, do *it* with thy might; for *there is* no work, nor device, nor knowledge, nor wisdom, in the grave, whither thou goest.

Nothing we do in this life will be carried on in Hell. As such, Christianity should not be just part of our lives. We need to serve our Lord with all of our life.

(Read Proverbs 7:23=27)

*****

APRIL 9

Philippians 3:13-14(KJV) (13) Brethren, I count not myself to have apprehended: but *this* one thing *I do*, forgetting those things which are behind, and reaching forth unto those things which are before, (14) I press toward the mark for the prize of the high calling of God in Christ Jesus.

Paul says here that he does not understand all things. But, there is one thing he does understand. He once thought he was serving God, but found out he really wasn't, and had to let it go. Now, he is reaching ahead to the high calling of God, and that it is through Jesus Christ and Him crucified. This reminds us that all of our attention must be on Jesus and what He did on Calvary.

(Read 1 Corinthians 9:24)

APRIL 10

Romans 6:13 (KJV) Neither yield ye your members *as* instruments of unrighteousness unto sin: but yield yourselves unto God, as those that are alive from the dead, and your members *as* instruments of righteousness unto God.

We must not surrender our bodies to the sin nature, but instead yield them to God. Yielding ourselves to Jesus and Him crucified guarantees that we will have victory over the sin nature. Because of Jesus, we are alive from the dead, we do not have to face the second death.

(Read Luke 9:23–24)

*****

APRIL 11

Matthew 10:32 (KJV) Whosoever therefore shall confess me before men, him will I confess also before my Father which is in heaven.

We are to witness to others about Jesus Christ and Him crucified. Jesus said if we would do that, then He will talk to the Father about us. What a wonderful promise!

(Read Revelation 3:5)

*****

APRIL 12

1 Thessalonians 5:22 (KJV) Abstain from all appearance of evil.

It is easy to know and understand that we should stay away from that which is actually evil. Did you know that if something just looks evil or wrong, that we should leave it alone also? Be careful, you do not want to lose your testimony.

(Read 1 Thessalonians 4:12)

*****

APRIL 13

Proverbs 4:23 (KJV) Keep thy heart with all diligence; for out of it *are* the issues of life.

We keep our heart, by keeping our faith in Jesus Christ and Him crucified. As long as we keep our faith there, then Satan cannot overcome us.

(Read 1 Corinthians 1:23-24)

*****

APRIL 14

John 5:39 (KJV) Search the scriptures; for in them ye think ye have eternal life: and they are they which testify of me.

It is not being suggested that we study the Scriptures, it is a command that we do so. In addition, we need to believe what they say. Let us not forget the entire story of the Bible is about Jesus and Him crucified.

(Read Luke 24:27)

*****

APRIL 15

Matthew 6:6 (KJV) But thou, when thou prayest, enter into thy closet, and when thou hast shut thy door, pray to thy Father which is in secret; and thy Father which seeth in secret shall reward thee openly.

Are you a sincere believer? If so, it is your duty to spend time in prayer with the Father. This is not to been done for show, that is for the benefit of man seeing what you are doing. We need to spend time alone with God. In doing so, we are making God's interests our own. Then God will make our interests His!

(Read 2 Kings 4:33)

*****

APRIL 16

1 Thessalonians 5:18 (KJV) In every thing give thanks: for this is the will of God in Christ Jesus concerning you.

Giving thanks should be a priority in our lives. Sometimes negative things come our way. Other times positive things come our way. Regardless, we should never fail to thank and praise God. Remember, this is the will of God.

(Read 2 Timothy 1:7)

*****

APRIL 17

Psalms 1:2 (KJV) But his delight *is* in the law of the LORD; and in his law doth he meditate day and night.

The Lord's delight is in God's Word. It was so even when He walked this earth. He is our example, and God's Word should also be the delight of our lives.

(Read Joshua 1:8)

*****

APRIL 18

2 Corinthians 13:5 (KJV) Examine yourselves, whether ye be in the faith; prove your own selves. Know ye not your own selves, how that Jesus Christ is in you, except ye be reprobates?

We need to examine ourselves on a daily basis. If we are to make sure we are in the faith, then we must make sure our faith is in Jesus and Him crucified. Then we will know, that Jesus Christ is in us. If He isn't in us, then we are rejected by Him.

(Read 1 Corinthians 9:27)

******

APRIL 19

Romans 12:3 (KJV) For I say, through the grace given unto me, to every man that is among you, not to think *of himself* more highly than he ought to think; but to think soberly, according as God hath dealt to every man the measure of faith.

We have what we have by the Grace of God. We should never have a prideful, unscriptural evaluation of ourselves. Remember, God has given to every man the measure of faith. It is given at the moment of conversion.

(Read 1 Corinthians 4:6)

APRIL 20

Isaiah 1:10 (KJV)
Hear the word of the LORD, ye rulers of Sodom; give ear unto the law of our God, ye people of Gomorrah.

In this verse, God is comparing Israel to the city of Sodom. Israel at that time was religious, but did not know God. Isaiah let them know they were an abomination to God. We too can be religious, without knowing God. We need to make sure that we are not religious, but saved by grace through the ***blood*** of Jesus Christ.

(Read 1 Samuel 15:22)

*****

APRIL 21

Proverbs 16:32 (KJV) *He that is* **slow to anger** *is* **better than the mighty; and he that ruleth his spirit than he that taketh a city.**

Only the Holy Ghost can bring true self control. Individuals cannot bring it about by themselves. It comes only by faith in Jesus and Him crucified.

(Read Galatians 2:20–21)

*****

APRIL 22

1 Corinthians 10:23 (KJV) All things are lawful for me, but all things are not expedient: all things are lawful for me, but all things edify not.

Paul is dealing with Christian liberty, and how it should work. Contrary to what the Corinthians thought then, and what many Christians think now, this freedom does not give us the right to do whatever we desire to do,

(Read Acts 9:31)

*****

APRIL 23

Hebrews 13:5 (KJV) *Let your* conversation *be* without covetousness; *and be* content with such things as ye have: for he hath said, I will never leave thee, nor forsake thee.

The word "conversation" as used here is referring to lifestyle. Our lifestyle should be without covetousness. Covetousness is a form of idolatry, and as such can separate us from God. We are to be content in all things, by being dependent on Jesus Christ. Jesus has made the promise that He will never leave or forsake us.

(Read Colossians 3:1-4)

*****

APRIL 24

Hebrews 10:36 (KJV)
For ye have need of patience, that, after ye have done the will of God, ye might receive the promise.

The Christian life should be a life of patience. Proper faith will always have proper patience. As a Christian, it is our duty to carry out the will of God. By carrying out the will of God in our lives, we have the assurance that we will receive the promise of God.

(Read Hebrews 9:15)

*****

APRIL 25

Ephesians 4:2 (KJV) With all lowliness and meekness, with longsuffering, forbearing one another in love;

All the things spoken of here, are works of the Holy Ghost. This means none of these can be accomplished in our own abilities. By keeping our faith in Jesus and His crucifixion, the help of the Holy Ghost will come to us.

(Read 1 Corinthians 1:17–18)

*****

APRIL 26

Luke 21:34(KJV) And take heed to yourselves, lest at any time your hearts be overcharged with surfeiting, and drunkenness, and cares of this life, and *so* that day come upon you unawares.

Are you ready for the Lord to come for you? He could come any time by death, or by the Rapture. Are you making sure your heart is right with the Lord? The word "overcharged" means to be weighed down. Three things are mentioned here that can weigh us down, and separate us from God. These things are excessive indulgence in sensual pleasures, drunkenness, and things in our lives that are not spiritual.

(Read Romans 13:13-14)

*****

APRIL 27

Titus 2:7 (KJV) In all things showing thyself a pattern of good works: in doctrine *showing* uncorruptness, gravity, sincerity,

We are to show ourselves an example of good works. Many times, our lives are the only Bibles that most people see. Our lives should show incorruptness, integrity, and sincerity. People need to see Jesus in us.

(Read 1 Timothy 4:13)

APRIL 28

Luke 12:37 (KJV) Blessed *are* those servants, whom the lord when he cometh shall find watching: verily I say unto you, that he shall gird himself, and make them to sit down to meat, and will come forth and serve them.

If we are watching, then we are ready for the rapture. After the rapture, the Lord will prepare the marriage supper of the Lamb. What a joyful time that will be. Just think about it, Jesus Himself will be the host of that special event.

(Read Matthew 24:42)

*****

APRIL 29

1 Thessalonians 4:11 (KJV) And that ye study to be quiet, and to do your own business, and to work with your own hands, as we commanded you;

Our goal in life should not to be prominently seen and heard. We should mind our own business, and not the business of others. As a Christian, we should work and not steal, and we should not be sponging off of others. Simply put, we should always be an example of Jesus Christ.

(Read 2 Thessalonians 3:12)

*****

APRIL 30

Philippians 3:12 (KJV) Not as though I had already attained, either were already perfect: but I follow after, if that I may apprehend that for which also I am apprehended of Christ Jesus.

The Apostle Paul writing to the Philippians is not claiming sinless perfection. Paul's goal is to pursue absolute Christ-likeness. He said he was saved by Jesus Christ for the purpose of being Christ like. We are saved for the same purpose.

(Read 1 Corinthians 9:24)

CHAPTER 5 - MAY

MAY 1

1 Peter 2:9 (KJV) But ye *are* a chosen generation, a royal priesthood, an holy nation, a peculiar people; that ye should show forth the praises of him who hath called you out of darkness into his marvellous light:

We have been chosen by God. A new race, if you will, made up of all who have accepted Jesus Christ. Due to being in Him, He has declared us to be kings and priests. He has made us a holy nation, which is basically a multitude of people who are of the same nature. Each one of us is a unique possession of God. All this is possible through the finished work of Christ at Calvary.

(Read Revelation 1:6)

*****

MAY 2

2 Timothy 2:19 (KJV) Nevertheless the foundation of God standeth sure, having this seal, The Lord knoweth them that are his. And, Let every one that nameth the name of Christ depart from iniquity.

Yes, our foundation is secure! We have been sealed by God, so we are protected by His hand. He guarantees both the security and the purity of the church. By keeping our faith in Jesus and His sacrifice, we are able to depart from iniquity (unrighteousness).

(Read Song of Solomon 8:6)

*****

MAY 3

Galatians 5:1 (KJV) Stand fast therefore in the liberty wherewith Christ hath made us free, and be not entangled again with the yoke of bondage.

The *blood* of Jesus has made us free! This is the freedom to live a holy life through Jesus and Him crucified. If we abandon God and stop serving Him, we once again enter into the bondage of the sin nature.

(Read Romans 6:18)

*****

MAY 4

Jude 1:3 (KJV) Beloved, when I gave all diligence to write unto you of the common salvation, it was needful for me to write unto you, and exhort *you* that ye should earnestly contend for the faith which was once delivered unto the saints.

Jude at first wanted to write about salvation, but the Spirit of God did not lead him in that direction. He felt the need to write something at once, but he needed the guidance of the Holy Ghost. He felt the saints needed to defend the doctrines of Christianity. We as the modern saints also need to defend the doctrines of Christianity, for those doctrines are under serious attack today.

(Read Philippians 1:27)

*****

MAY 5

Hebrews 10:24 KJV) And let us consider one another to provoke unto love and to good works:

Let us think carefully about each other. How should we treat our brothers and sisters in the Lord? We should treat them with love, and show them good works. This is how we expect to be treated ourselves, and so it is what others expect of us. This comes from someone who has true faith in Jesus and His sacrifice for us.

(Read Hebrews 3:13)

MAY 6

Hebrews 10:25 (KJV) Not forsaking the assembling of ourselves together, as the manner of some *is*; but exhorting *one another*: and so much the more, as ye see the day approaching.

it is important for Christians to assemble together to worship. We draw strength from one another for one thing. In addition the Word of God declares that when two or three are gathered together in the name of Jesus, He is in the midst. We also have the opportunity to encourage each other in the faith, which is very important. Finally, we need to do so, because we are living in the last days.

(Read Romans 13:11)

*****

MAY 7

2 Corinthians 13:11 (KJV) Finally, brethren, farewell. Be perfect, be of good comfort, be of one mind, live in peace; and the God of love and peace shall be with you.

The word "perfect" as used here is meaning "mature". So first of all, Paul is speaking here of the need to be mature in the Lord. We are to be comforted in the Lord, and to have the mind of the Lord in all things. Finally, we are to live in the peace of God. All of this can take place as long as we have faith in Jesus Christ, and His work at Calvary.

(Read Romans 15:33)

MAY 8

Psalms 122:7 (KJV) Peace be within thy walls, *and* prosperity within thy palaces.

We are to remember to pray for the peace of Jerusalem. This verse is even telling us how to pray. Let us not forget Jerusalem is the center of the earth, and the place God chose to put His name.

(Read 1 Samuel 25:6)

*****

MAY 9

Ephesians 5:2 (KJV) And walk in love, as Christ also hath loved us, and hath given himself for us an offering and a sacrifice to God for a sweetsmelling savour.

The word "walk" is referring to our behavior. Our normal everyday behavior should be showing everyone the love of God. Jesus was our offering, and sacrifice. He fulfilled all of the blood offerings found in the Book of Leviticus. He did this by becoming the offering for sin on the cross. He was the supreme sacrifice accepted by God in our place.

(Read Philippians 4:18)

*****

MAY 10

1 Peter 5:5 (KJV) Likewise, ye younger, submit yourselves unto the elder. Yea, all *of you* be subject one to another, and be clothed with humility: for God resisteth the proud, and giveth grace to the humble.

The younger ones in the Lord should be willing to be led and taught by the older Christians. Older Christians should be willing to work with younger Christians. We should all have a mutual understanding. Humility is the virtue that we will all have if we keep our faith in Jesus and Him crucified. God simply does not like a proud person. God gives grace to those who practice humility.

(Read James 4:10)

*****

MAY 11

Philippians 2:3 (KJV) *Let* nothing *be done* through strife or vainglory; but in lowliness of mind let each esteem other better than themselves.

We should not do anything through quarreling and boasting. This is simply the wrong attitude. Our attitude in all things should be one of humility. This humility will show when we prefer others over ourselves.

(Read Ephesians 4:1-3)

MAY 12

Colossians 3:13 (KJV) Forbearing one another, and forgiving one another, if any man have a quarrel against any: even as Christ forgave you, so also *do* ye.

We should be exhibiting patience with each other, as well as forgiving each other. This will help us to quickly end any disagreement that comes our way. Let us remember, that Jesus forgave us, and we should be willing to forgive others.

(Read Ephesians 4:32)

*****

MAY 13

Matthew 7:1-3 (KJV) (1) Judge not, that ye be not judged. (2) For with what judgment ye judge, ye shall be judged: and with what measure ye mete, it shall be measured to you again. (3) And why beholdest thou the mote that is in thy brother's eye, but considerest not the beam that is in thine own eye?

This is a Scripture that many people quote today, but for the most part it is being used incorrectly. Many who quote it today, are using it as an excuse to continue doing things they know they should not be doing. Judging has to do with passing judgment. We are not to pass judgment on someone as to where they spend eternity. But, on the other hand, the Bible does tell us if we see a brother who is at fault (sinning), that we are to go them and speak to them, for the purpose of

71

restoration.

(Read 1 Corinthians 4:3)

*****

MAY 14

Ephesians 4:32 (KJV) And be ye kind one to another, tenderhearted, forgiving one another, even as God for Christ's sake hath forgiven you.

We are to be kind to each other, and tenderhearted. In addition, we need to be quick to forgive each other. Jesus set the example, by forgiving us, when we were unforgivable. As he forgives us, let us forgive others.

(Read Colossians 3:12-13)

*****

MAY 15

Romans 15:14 (KJV) And I myself also am persuaded of you, my brethren, that ye also are full of goodness, filled with all knowledge, able also to admonish one another.

Paul shows that he had faith in the Romans he was speaking to. He spoke of them having goodness because of their knowledge of Jesus Christ. He spoke of them having knowledge of the Word of God. He went on to say they could correct each other if need be, because of their knowledge of the Word. These Romans were setting an example that we need to follow today.

(Read Galatians 5:22-23)

*****

MAY 16

1 Thessalonians 5:11 (KJV) Wherefore comfort yourselves together, and edify one another, even as also ye do.

We are to comfort one another with thoughts of the coming Rapture. Knowing, that the Rapture will keep us from the wrath of God that will be poured out on this world during the great tribulation. In addition, we should be cheering and strengthening one another.

(Read Acts 9:31)

*****

MAY 17

James 5:16 (KJV) Confess *your* faults one to another, and pray one for another, that ye may be healed. The effectual fervent prayer of a righteous man availeth much.

We need to be quick to admit a fault, instead of hiding the fault. We should be praying for each other for healing. It doesn't matter if it is a preacher, a deacon, or a layman praying, if you have a correct relationship with God, then God will hear and answer the prayer.

(Read 1 Timothy 2:1)

*****

MAY 18

Philippians 3:16 (KJV) Nevertheless, whereto we have already attained, let us walk by the same rule, let us mind the same thing.

Let us not forget the life we should be living, being an example of Jesus Christ. That path we are to walk, is having faith in Jesus, and what He did for us at Calvary.

(Read Luke 9:23–24)

*****

MAY 19

1 Corinthians 1:10 (KJV) Now I beseech you, brethren, by the name of our Lord Jesus Christ, that ye all speak the same thing, and *that* there be no divisions among you; but *that* ye be perfectly joined together in the same mind and in the same judgment.

Paul is begging his brethren at this time. Paul reminds them that they should all be preaching the doctrine of salvation, which is Jesus and Him crucified. There should be no division between us, but unity in the fact that Jesus died in our place, to provide complete and total victory to us. We are to be joined together in one faith. This can only be accomplished by having faith in Jesus and Him crucified.

(Read Luke 6:40)

*****

MAY 20

Matthew 18:20 (KJV) For where two or three are gathered together in my name, there am I in the midst of them.

Oh, the importance of us assembling together with other Christians. If we meet in His name, with two or three people, He has promised to be in our presence. This happens because in God's eyes, this is a church.

(Read Matthew 28:19-20)

*****

MAY 21

Colossians 3:16 (KJV) Let the word of Christ dwell in you richly in all wisdom; teaching and admonishing one another in psalms and hymns and spiritual songs, singing with grace in your hearts to the Lord.

We are to allow the Word of God to be one with us, always knowing that Jesus and His death on Calvary has brought complete and total victory to us, in all things. We are to teach and encourage each other, with Psalms, hymns, and spiritual songs. The songs that we sing, should be meant to worship the Lord.

(Read Ephesians 4:29)

*****

MAY 22

Ephesians 4:29 (KJV) Let no corrupt communication proceed out of your mouth, but that which is good to the use of edifying, that it may minister grace unto the hearers.

As Christians, we should be very careful about what we say. No slander or faithlessness should come out of our mouths. The things that we say should be to build up others, and not to tear them down. We should be a blessing to everyone around us.

(Read Colossians 4:6)

*****

MAY 23

Romans 15:1 (KJV) We then that are strong ought to bear the infirmities of the weak, and not to please ourselves.

This is talking about being weak in the Faith and strong in the Faith. It should be the goal of those who are strong in the Faith to help those who are not. In doing so, the weak will also become strong in Faith and knowledge of the Word of God. Remember, if we are only interested in pleasing ourselves, we will ruin our Christian fellowship and testimony.

(Read Romans 14:19)

*****

MAY 24

Hebrews 13:3 (KJV) Remember them that are in bonds, as bound with them; *and* them which suffer adversity, as being yourselves also in the body.

This verse is referring to Christians who were imprisoned for their Faith. We are to become one with them, and not forgetting to pray for them. He goes on to refer to the body of Christ, the Church. When one member of the body suffers, in a sense, we all suffer.

(Read Romans 12:15)

*****

MAY 25

Galatians 6:10 (KJV) As we have therefore opportunity, let us do good unto all *men*, especially unto them who are

of the household of faith.

If our faith is in Jesus and Him crucified, then the Holy Ghost will help us do good to all men. There are many Christians who do not understand the Faith. Because of this, they are constantly walking in defeat. We are to share with them how Jesus provided us with complete and total victory when He died on the cross.

(Read Romans 8:2)

*****

MAY 26

Galatians 6:1 (KJV) Brethren, if a man be overtaken in a fault, ye which are spiritual, restore such an one in the spirit of meekness; considering thyself, lest thou also be tempted.

This verse is speaking of moral failure. This comes about when someone ignorantly places themselves under the Law. This will guarantee failure. We who understand the total victory provided by Jesus and Him crucified, can help that person by sharing with him about the victory provided by the crucifixion. Only the Holy Ghost can provide victory, and that can only be done by having faith in the sacrifice of Jesus. We should always have a proper attitude, one that is not overbearing, or holier than thou. We must always remember that if not careful, we can open the door for Satan to attack us also.

(Read 1 Corinthians 10:12)

*****

MAY 27

James 4:11 (KJV) Speak not evil one of another, brethren. He that speaketh evil of *his* brother, and judgeth his brother, speaketh evil of the law, and judgeth the law: but if thou judge the law, thou art not a doer of the law, but a judge.

We should be very careful in reference to what we say about each other. We are not to be self-appointed judges. When we begin to judge others by the Law, then we bring ourselves under the Law. In doing so, we will only find condemnation, and such a person has placed themselves in the position of God.

(Read 1 Peter 2:1)

*****

MAY 28

1 Thessalonians 5:12-13 (KJV) (12) And we beseech you, brethren, to know them which labour among you, and are over you in the Lord, and admonish you; (13) And to esteem them very highly in love for their work's sake. *And* be at peace among yourselves.

You should know the preacher you are following is actually preaching the Word of God. If they are truly preaching the Word of God, then they should be highly respected for the work they do. The respect that you have will help produce peace among each other.

(Read 1 Timothy 5:17)

*****

MAY 29

Ephesians 6:18-19 (KJV) (18) Praying always with all prayer and supplication in the Spirit, and watching thereunto with all perseverance and supplication for all saints; (19) And for me, that utterance may be given unto me, that I may open my mouth boldly, to make known the mystery of the Gospel,

We should be continually praying, until our prayer is answered. As we pray, we should be very sensitive to the desires of the Holy Ghost. We need to be persistent with our requests and petitions. The saints of God should be praying for each other. Paul desired prayer, as we should, that we would be fearless and confident in presenting the Gospel, and properly preaching and teaching the New Testament, which is the story of Jesus and Him crucified.

(Read Jude 1:20)

*****

MAY 30

Hebrews 3:12 (KJV) Take heed, brethren, lest there be in any of you an evil heart of unbelief, in departing from the living God.

We should listen closely to what Paul has to say here. It is possible to develop a heart of unbelief and stop serving God. He is talking about losing belief in Jesus and Him crucified.

(Read Hebrews 10:24-25)

*****

MAY 31

Hebrews 12:15 (KJV) Looking diligently lest any man fail of the grace of God; lest any root of bitterness springing up trouble *you*, and thereby many be defiled;

If we fail to function within the Grace of God, we can fall from Grace. If we try to live for God outside of believing in Jesus and Him crucified, we will bring failure and the roots of bitterness into our lives, and even make ourselves filthy in the sight of God.

(Read Galatians 5:19–21)

*****

CHAPTER 6 - JUNE

JUNE 1

Matthew 5:13 (KJV)
Ye are the salt of the earth: but if the salt have lost his savour, wherewith shall it be salted? It is thenceforth good for nothing, but to be cast out, and to be trodden under foot of men.

We are the salt, or preservative God has sent to this earth. Salt is used here as a type of the Word of God. God wants us to be filled with His Word, but He does not expect us to keep it to ourselves. He expects us to share it with others. But, if we don't keep filled up with God's Word, we are no longer any use to God or man.

(Read Mark 9:50)

*****

JUNE 2

Matthew 5:14 (KJV) Ye are the light of the world. A city that is set on an hill cannot be hid.

We are a reflection of the light that comes from Jesus Christ. True light cannot and will not be hid. Just as a true Christian cannot hide the fact he is a Christian. In addition, a true Christian cannot help but share his love for Christ.

(Read Philippians 2:15)

*****

JUNE 3

Matthew 7:12 (KJV) Therefore all things whatsoever ye would that men should do to you, do ye even so to them: for this is the law and the prophets.

This is what we call the Golden Rule. It speaks of what is reasonably and morally helpful and controlled by using Jesus Christ as our example. This is actually the sum of all Bible teaching.

(Read Luke 13:24)

*****

JUNE 4

1 Peter 2:11 (KJV) Dearly beloved, I beseech *you* as strangers and pilgrims, abstain from fleshly lusts, which war against the soul;

We are not really a pilgrim in the Biblical since, unless we first become a stranger to this world. We must remember that the "sin nature" is still with us, and as such, we must keep our faith in Jesus and Him crucified,

(Read James 4:1)

*****

JUNE 5

1 Corinthians 15:58 (KJV) Therefore, my beloved brethren, be ye stedfast, unmoveable, always abounding in the work of the Lord, forasmuch as ye know that your labour is not in vain in the Lord.

We should be established in the Word of God, with our faith firmly on Jesus and Him crucified. We should not allow our faith to be shaken loose from it either. It should always be our goal to share the Lord and His sacrifice with others. Always remember, our witnessing about the victory at the cross will always bring wonderful results.

(Read 1 Corinthians 1:18)

*****

JUNE 6

Matthew 6:24 (KJV) No man can serve two masters: for either he will hate the one, and love the other; or else he will hold to the one, and despise the other. Ye cannot serve God and mammon.

It is absolutely impossible to serve two masters. Either we are totally sold out to God, or totally sold out to Satan. It is either God or worldly gain.

(Read Galatians 1:10)

*****

JUNE 7

Matthew 5:16 (KJV) Let your light so shine before men, that they may see your good works, and glorify your Father which is in heaven.

How do we let our light shine? The answer is proper faith. If we have proper faith, then it will produce proper works. On the other hand though, proper works will not produce proper faith. Proper works will always glorify God, but improper works will only glorify man.

(Read 1 Peter 2:12)

*****

JUNE 8

Romans 12:18 (KJV) If it be possible, as much as lieth in you, live peaceably with all men.

Although we do not have any control over the conduct of other people, God expects us to take the first step in keeping peace. The Christian should never work to disturb the peace.

(Read 2 Corinthians 13:11)

*****

JUNE 9

James 2:8 (KJV) If ye fulfil the royal law according to the scripture, Thou shalt love thy neighbour as thyself, ye do well:

The Royal Law. You shall love your neighbor as yourself. It is up to us to show favor to everyone, regardless of their station in life.

(Read Romans 13:9)

*****

JUNE 10

Romans 15:2 (KJV) Let every one of us please *his* neighbour for *his* good to edification.

We should be aware of the younger Christians around us. Being aware of them includes not doing something they think is wrong, even if we do not believe it is. We need to think about what is good for them.

(Read Romans 14:19)

*****

JUNE 11

1 Thessalonians 3:12 (KJV) And the Lord make you to increase and abound in love one toward another, and toward all *men*, even as we *do* toward you:

God's desire is for us to continually increase and abound in love for each other. He even desires for us to increase and abound in love toward all men everywhere. The more we understand the sacrifice of Jesus on the cross, the more this will happen in our lives.

(Read 1 Thessalonians 4:1)

*****

JUNE 12

James 5:20 (KJV) Let him know, that he which converteth the sinner from the error of his way shall save a soul from death, and shall hide a multitude of sins.

Our purpose on earth other than worshiping God, is to reach the lost and undone. James reminds us here, that if a sinner turns from his wicked ways because of our efforts, that we have saved a soul from eternal torment. We can accomplish this by sharing the death, burial, and resurrection of Jesus.

(Read Romans 4:7)

*****

JUNE 13

Romans 13:7 (KJV) Render therefore to all their dues: tribute to whom tribute *is due*; custom to whom custom; fear to whom fear; honour to whom honour.

Paul lets the Romans know that it is right and proper for Christians to pay taxes. He goes a step farther and says if we owe anything, that we ought to pay it. Even hidden taxes are to be paid. Government as an institution should be respected, as well as civil servants from the lowest to the highest.

(Read Matthew 22:21)

*****

JUNE 14

Philippians 2:15 (KJV)
That ye may be blameless and harmless, the sons of God,
without rebuke, in the midst of a crooked and perverse
nation, among whom ye shine as lights in the world;

God desires for us as sons of God to be blameless and harmless. We should be living a life for God that cannot be criticized, even if we live in an ungodly place. As saints of God, we are to be lights to the world. All of this can only take place as long as we continue to have faith in Jesus and Him crucified.

(Read 2 Peter 3:14)

*****

JUNE 15

Ephesians 5:15-16 (KJV) See then that ye walk
circumspectly, not as fools, but as wise, Redeeming the
time, because the days are evil.

As a Christian, we are to live our lives carefully and paying attention to the Word of God. We should not be like a person who will not serve God. We should do our best to draw close to God. We should take advantage of every opportunity the Lord brings our way. We are facing evil days, as such, Jesus Christ and Him crucified needs to be our one and only foundation, so we can do the things God wants us to do.

(Read Romans 13:11)

*****

JUNE 16

Psalms 112:5 (KJV) A good man showeth favour, and lendeth: he will guide his affairs with discretion.

A good man is someone who serves the Lord with their entire heart. God will bless those who trust Him and live for Him He will also guide them in His ways.

(Read Psalm 55:22)

*****

JUNE 17

Philippians 4:5 (KJV) Let your moderation be known unto all men. The Lord *is* at hand.

We as Christians are to be satisfied with what we have, and people will take note of it. The Lord is always near us, and His coming is nearer than we can even imagine.

(Read James 3:17)

JUNE 18

Romans 12:19 (KJV) Dearly beloved, avenge not yourselves, but *rather* give place unto wrath: for it is written, Vengeance *is* mine; I will repay, saith the Lord.

It is not the place of a Christian to take vengeance on fellow human beings. This belongs to God and God alone. It is not our place to take God's work out of His hands.

(Read Hebrews 10:30)

*****

JUNE 19

Ephesians 4:28 (KJV) Let him that stole steal no more: but rather let him labour, working with *his* hands the thing which is good, that he may have to give to him that needeth.

As Christians, our high moral standards keep us from doing that which is evil. We are to labor and work for what we have. Because of this, we have the ability to give to those who are in need.

(Read Acts 20:35)

*****

JUNE 20

1 Thessalonians 4:12 (KJV) That ye may walk honestly toward them that are without, and *that* ye may have lack of nothing.

As Christians, our lives should be setting an example for unbelievers. Always remember, if we follow the Lord with our whole heart, He will be sure to provide for us.

(Read Romans 13:13-14)

*****

JUNE 21

Luke 16:10 (KJV) He that is faithful in that which is least is faithful also in much: and he that is unjust in the least is unjust also in much.

This Scripture implies that if a Christian is faithful with the little things God gives Him, then he will be faithful in everything God gives him. But on the other hand, if a Christian does not properly handle the small things God gives him, he will be unjust in everything, which includes spiritual matters.

(Read Matthew 25:21)

*****

JUNE 22

Ephesians 4:25 (KJV) Wherefore putting away lying, speak every man truth with his neighbour: for we are members one of another.

The first thing that a Christian should stop doing, is telling lies. This also includes believing in something other than Jesus and Him crucified. Remember, anything other than Christ and Him crucified is a lie. Christians should always make a point of telling the truth, and the ultimate truth is the plan of salvation. This brings about true righteousness and holiness. Since we are members of one another, we should all share the Good News of Jesus Death, Burial, and Resurrection.

(Read Romans 12:5)

*****

JUNE 23

Titus 3:2 (KJV) To speak evil of no man, to be no brawlers, *but* gentle, showing all meekness unto all men.

Titus continues our education concerning how to live our Christian life. The first thing he states is that we should not speak evil of anyone. We should not be causing disputes and quarreling. But, we should allow the Fruit of the Spirit to be in operation in our life. All this is brought about by our faith in Jesus and Him crucified.

(Read Galatians 5:22–23)

JUNE 24

James 1:27(KJV) Pure religion and undefiled before God and the Father is this, To visit the fatherless and widows in their affliction, *and* to keep himself unspotted from the world.

Pure religion is speaking to our spirituality. As a Christian our desire should be to do everything we can to please God. As we have said before, pure faith will cause us to have proper works. Proper faith will also cause us to have complete victory in our lives, through the power of the Holy Ghost.

(Read Ephesians 5:20-21)

*****

JUNE 25

Romans 12:20-21(KJV) (20) Therefore if thine enemy hunger, feed him; if he thirst, give him drink: for in so doing thou shalt heap coals of fire on his head. (21) Be not overcome of evil, but overcome evil with good.

Contrary to the thoughts of the world, we are to treat our enemies well. By being good to our enemies, we are showing mercy to them, as God showed mercy to us. Evil produces more evil, as such, we are not to allow evil to become a part of us. By treating the evil person well, we can win them over to Christ.

(Read Matthew 5:44)

*****

JUNE 26

Galatians 6:9(KJV) And let us not be weary in well doing: for in due season we shall reap, if we faint not.

We should not grow weary in serving God. If we keep our faith in Jesus and Him crucified, we shall receive the rewards found in the Word of God. Do not give up, the promises are yours. Jesus never fails.

(Read Luke 18:1)

*****

JUNE 27

Titus 3:1 (KJV) Put them in mind to be subject to principalities and powers, to obey magistrates, to be ready to every good work,

As Christians, we are under the authority of civil governments, as long as they do not go against the Word of God. We should always look for the opportunity to do that which is good.

(Read 2 Timothy 3:17)

*****

JUNE 28

Philippians 4:8 (KJV) Finally, brethren, whatsoever things are true, whatsoever things *are* honest, whatsoever things *are* just, whatsoever things *are* pure, whatsoever thing *are* lovely, whatsoever things *are* of good report; if *there be* any virtue, and if *there be* any praise, think on these things.

Have you ever thought on what we Christians should be thinking about? That's right, good things. It can be done when we have faith in Jesus and what He did for us at Calvary.

(Read 2 Corinthians 6:6-7)

*****

JUNE 29

Luke 17:10(KJV) So likewise ye, when ye shall have done all those things which are commanded you, say, We are unprofitable servants: we have done that which was our duty to do.

Never think more highly of yourself than you ought to think. It is only through Jesus that we are anything.

(Read Matthew 25:21)

*****

JUNE 30

1 Corinthians 6:19-20 (KJV) (19) What? know ye not that your body is the temple of the Holy Ghost *which is* in you, which ye have of God, and ye are not your own? (20) For ye are bought with a price: therefore glorify God in your body, and in your spirit, which are God's.

Don't you know that your body is the Temple of the Holy Ghost? That is right, the body of the Christian is the Temple of the Holy Ghost. We as Christians do not belong to ourselves, we belong to God. We were purchased by the ***Blood*** of Jesus Christ. We are to glorify God with our body and with our spirit, because we were created by God, and purchased at a great cost.

(Read 1 Corinthians 7:23-24)

*****

CHAPTER 7 - JULY

JULY 1

Psalms 5:11 (KJV) But let all those that put their trust in thee rejoice: let them ever shout for joy, because thou defendest them: let them also that love thy name be joyful in thee.

We have something to shout about. We have something to rejoice in. We can do it because of what God has done for us in this present life. We can also do it because of the coming future He has promised us. It is all ours, because of the shed *blood* at Calvary!

(Read 1 Samuel 2:1)

*****

JULY 2

Philippians 3:3 (KJV) For we are the circumcision, which worship God in the spirit, and rejoice in Christ Jesus, and have no confidence in the flesh.

We are the circumcision is referring to the circumcision of the heart. This means that we are saved by faith in Jesus and His sacrifice at Calvary. Because of this, we worship by and through the Spirit of God. We can rejoice in Christ Jesus, because we do not have any confidence in the flesh. Our confidence is in Jesus and Him crucified.

(Read Galatians 6:14)

*****

JULY 3

Romans 14:17 (KJV) For the kingdom of God is not meat and drink; but righteousness, and peace, and joy in the Holy Ghost.

The Kingdom of God has nothing to do with buildings, rules, regulations, ceremonies, or even rituals. It has to do with righteousness, peace, and joy. All of this is controlled by the Holy Ghost, who produces these characteristics within God's children.

(Read Romans 12:12-13)

*****

JULY 4

Psalms 89:15 (KJV) Blessed *is* the people that know the joyful sound: they shall walk, O LORD, in the light of thy countenance.

These are the people who truly know God. They have been washed in the ***blood*** of the Lamb. They are in Jesus, and Jesus is in them. They hear and know the joyful sound. They walk in the light of His countenance because of Jesus and Him crucified.

(Read Psalm 4:6)

*****

JULY 5

Romans 5:11 (KJV) And not only *so*, but we also joy in God through our Lord Jesus Christ, by whom we have now received the atonement.

We have been reconciled to God, which is something to brag about. This means God has re-established a close relationship with us, through the ***blood*** of His Son, Jesus Christ.

(Read 1 Corinthians 1:31)

*****

JULY 6

Jeremiah 15:16 (KJV) Thy words were found, and I did eat them; and thy word was unto me the joy and rejoicing of mine heart: for I am called by thy name, O LORD God of hosts.

As a Christian, we should have a great love of God. We should also love God's word so much, that we desire to consume It. As we read and study God's Word, we grow closer to Him. We then want to rejoice that we are called by His name.

(Read Psalm 119:111)

*****

JULY 7

Psalms 118:24 (KJV) This *is* the day *which* the LORD hath made; we will rejoice and be glad in it.

God has made this very day. It is within His hands, for it belongs to Him. This gives us even more to rejoice about.

(Read Numbers 6:27)

*****

JULY 8

1 Peter 1:8 (KJV) Whom having not seen, ye love; in whom, though now ye see *him* not, yet believing, ye rejoice with joy unspeakable and full of glory:

We haven't seen Jesus, yet we still love Him. This is because the Holy Ghost has made Him real in our hearts. We need to have total and complete faith in the Lord, although we have never seen Him. When we do, we will begin to rejoice with joy unspeakable and full of glory.

(Read Romans 6:22)

*****

JULY 9

Psalms 32:1-2 (KJV) (1) Blessed *is he whose* transgression *is* forgiven, *whose* sin *is* covered. (2) Blessed *is* the man unto whom the LORD imputeth not iniquity, and in whose spirit *there is* no guile.

There is terror in unconfessed sin. That is why a person is so blessed when their sins are forgiven. Although we are guilty, when we truly repent, then God forgives us, and those sins we once had, are never remembered by God again.

(Read 2 Corinthians 5:19)

*****

JULY 10

Romans 5:2 (KJV) By whom also we have access by faith into this grace wherein we stand, and rejoice in hope of the glory of God.

By faith in Jesus Christ, we have access to God's grace. This is the only way we can stand before God. In addition, we are guaranteed the hope of eternal life. All this brings glory to God.

(Read Hebrews 3:6)

*****

JULY 11

Psalms 128:1-2 (KJV) (1) Blessed *is* every one that feareth the LORD; that walketh in his ways. (2) For thou shalt eat the labour of thine hands: happy *shalt* thou *be*, and *it shall be* well with thee.

We are blessed. Those that walk in God's ways, and who look at God as a child looks at their parent, are blessed. He shall always provide for you, and you shall not want for anything.

(Read Psalm 112:1)

*****

JULY 12

Psalms 119:47 (KJV) And I will delight myself in thy commandments, which I have loved.

David shows us the way to God's heart with this verse. When we delight ourselves in God's Word, love Him with our whole heart, and love not the things of this world, then we have found the heart of God.

(Read Psalm 119:16)

*****

JULY 13

Psalms 4:6-7 (KJV) (6) *There be* many that say, Who will show us *any* good? LORD, lift thou up the light of thy countenance upon us. (7) Thou hast put gladness in my heart, more than in the time *that* their corn and their wine increased.

What is it that man is always looking for, and never finding? They are looking for what is good, but for the most part, they do not look in the right direction. True good is to have the countenance of God shining on us. We must never forget that the blessings of God are much greater than we can receive from the material world.

(Read Psalm 31:16)

*****

JULY 14

Psalms 16:2-3 (KJV) (2) *O my soul*, **thou hast said unto the LORD, Thou** *art* **my Lord: my goodness** *extendeth* **not to thee; (3)** *But* **to the saints that** *are* **in the earth, and** *to* **the excellent, in whom** *is* **all my delight.**

This is how we should actually feel about the Lord. Listen to what is being said. "You are my Lord; there is no good in me, other than from you. You are my only good." To us, the children of God, He is our delight. He is our Messiah. He is our deliverer.

(Read Isaiah 62:4)

*****

JULY 15

Isaiah 56:7 (KJV) Even them will I bring to my holy mountain, and make them joyful in my house of prayer: their burnt offerings and their sacrifices *shall be* **accepted upon mine altar; for mine house shall be called an house of prayer for all people.**

This is a prophecy about what God would do in the future. It speaks of God providing a supreme sacrifice to bring man back into fellowship with Him. Isaiah was looking forward to all of this. We who are Christians are looking back to it. Together, we look at Calvary, which provides it all.

(Read Hebrews 13:15)

JULY 16

Psalms 20:5 (KJV) We will rejoice in thy salvation, and in the name of our God we will set up *our* banners: the LORD fulfil all thy petitions.

The thought is, if the sacrifice of Jesus Christ is accepted, then the salvation of everyone who puts their trust in that sacrifice will be accepted. Well, the sacrifice of Jesus was accepted. Because of this, we can rejoice with joy unspeakable, and full of glory.

(Read Psalm 9:14)

*****

JULY 17

Psalms 90:14 (KJV) O satisfy us early with thy mercy; that we may rejoice and be glad all our days.

The only satisfaction there is, is from God. We can rejoice and be glad, because of His mercy, and His grace.

(Read Psalm 85:6)

*****

JULY 18

2 Corinthians 1:12 (KJV) For our rejoicing is this, the testimony of our conscience, that in simplicity and godly sincerity, not with fleshly wisdom, but by the grace of God, we have had our conversation in the world, and more abundantly to you-ward.

We can boast in the Lord, because He gives us a good conscience. The simplicity of God is His simple plan of salvation, which is the shed blood of Calvary. It has nothing to do with worldly wisdom, for that can do nothing for us. It simply takes the grace of God.

(Read 1 Corinthians 5:8)

*****

JULY 19

Acts 20:35 (KJV) I have showed you all things, how that so labouring ye ought to support the weak, and to remember the words of the Lord Jesus, how he said, It is more blessed to give than to receive.

We need to remember our Christian walk should be setting an example of Jesus Christ to others. In doing so, we are giving of ourselves to others, to give them the opportunity for salvation, and growing closer to the Lord.

(Read 1 Thessalonians 5:14)

JULY 20

Romans 5:3-4 (KJV) (3) And not only *so*, but we glory in tribulations also: knowing that tribulation worketh patience; (4) And patience, experience; and experience, hope:

First, we need to realize that tribulations do not hurt us. In fact, if we keep our faith in Jesus and Him crucified, then we actually grow in the Lord. We can then look back at the experience, and remember how the Lord delivered us.

(Read 1 Peter 3:14)

*****

JULY 21

Joel 2:26 (KJV) And ye shall eat in plenty, and be satisfied, and praise the name of the LORD your God, that hath dealt wondrously with you: and my people shall never be ashamed.

One of the "perks" of being a child of God, is that He takes care of us. He will provide our needs, whether they be spiritual or physical. He is faithful to those who are faithful to Him. Because of this, we will always have reason to praise Him.

(Read Isaiah 49:23)

*****

JULY 22

Proverbs 10:22 (KJV) The blessing of the LORD, it maketh rich, and he addeth no sorrow with it.

As children of God, we are rich. It may not be money, although it could be. We are rich in fellowship with Him and with other Christians. We are rich in God. We are rich in so many different ways, especially when you consider there is no sorrow in Him.

(Read Proverbs 3:33)

*****

JULY 23

Psalms 63:7 (KJV) Because thou hast been my help, therefore in the shadow of thy wings will I rejoice.

God is our help at all times, not just in times of need. I am convinced many times He is working behind the scenes, in the spirit world, protecting us when we don't even know it. As such, we can always rest in Him.

(Read Ruth 2:12)

*****

JULY 24

Ecclesiastes 9:7 (KJV) Go thy way, eat thy bread with joy, and drink thy wine with a merry heart; for God now accepteth thy works.

If we will accept God's will in our lives, and serve Him with our whole heart, then we will produce works for Him. God then accepts those works, for they are done for the right reasons. Because of this, there will be joy and a merry heart on our part.

(Read 1 Samuel 1:18)

*****

JULY 25

Psalms 30:5 (KJV) For his anger *endureth but* a moment; in his favour *is* life: weeping may endure for a night, but joy *cometh* in the morning.

God's anger with us is over when we accept Jesus Christ as our Saviour. There may be times later in our life when the enemy comes against us and causes problems. But, we can rejoice in the fact in knowing the trial will soon be over, for God delivers His children from the clutches of Satan. God is always right on time.

(Read Psalm 126:5)

*****

JULY 26

Psalms 32:11 (KJV) Be glad in the LORD, and rejoice, ye righteous: and shout for joy, all *ye that are* upright in heart.

The true Christian is the only one in this world that has anything to shout about. This is because we know we belong to God, and He always takes care of us.

(Read Deuteronomy 32:43)

*****

JULY 27

John 16:24 (KJV) Hitherto have ye asked nothing in my name: ask, and ye shall receive, that your joy may be full.

As children of God, we have the authority to speak to God, and to ask things of God. When we ask something of God, we are to ask in Jesus name. When doing this, we need to understand that all things are given to us through and by what Jesus did on the cross of Calvary. When we properly understand what Jesus did for us on the cross, then and only then can our joy be full.

(Read John 15:11)

*****

JULY 28

Psalms 65:4 (KJV) Blessed *is the man whom* thou choosest, and causest to approach *unto thee, that* he may dwell in thy courts: we shall be satisfied with the goodness of thy house, *even* of thy holy temple.

The Lord chooses those who accept Him. He has made it possible for us to enter into the Holy of Holies. He is satisfied with our goodness, because we have been covered with the **blood** of Jesus. It is the goodness or righteousness we have received from Jesus, nothing we have done in ourselves. Once we enter into eternity, then we will enter into God's Holy Temple in Heaven.

(Read Psalm 27:4)

*****

JULY 29

John 15:11 (KJV) These things have I spoken unto you, that my joy might remain in you, and *that* your joy might be full.

As long as our faith remains in Jesus and Him crucified, then the joy of the Lord will remain in us. Once I properly understand Jesus, and what He did for us on the cross, then our joy can be full.

(Read 1 John 1:4)

JULY 30

Luke 2:29-30 (KJV) (29) Lord, now lettest thou thy servant depart in peace, according to thy word: (30) For mine eyes have seen thy salvation,

This portion of Scripture indicates that it had been many years since the Lord showed Simeon he would see the Messiah. He did not have to ask anyone who the child was, he recognized Him immediately. Once we see Him, we also know Him, for Jesus is our salvation.

(Read John 9:37-38)

*****

JULY 31

Matthew 25:21 (KJV) His lord said unto him, Well done, *thou* good and faithful servant: thou hast been faithful over a few things, I will make thee ruler over many things: enter thou into the joy of thy lord.

God wants us to be faithful unto Him. He has not called us to be successful in this world, He has called us to be faithful to Him.

(Read Hebrews 12:2)

*****

CHAPTER 8 - AUGUST

AUGUST 1

John 16:33 (KJV) These things I have spoken unto you, that in me ye might have peace. In the world ye shall have tribulation: but be of good cheer; I have overcome the world.

Things at times will look terrible. In fact we can appear to be facing utter defeat, but things are not always as they appear. Jesus is still in control, regardless of what things look like. He has everything under control. In this world we will face tribulation, but Jesus has overcome the world. He did it 2,000 years ago as he hung on the cross, and declared, "It is finished".

(Read Ephesians 2:14)

*****

AUGUST 2

Psalms 51:12 (KJV) Restore unto me the joy of thy salvation; and uphold me *with thy* free spirit.

One of the jobs of the Holy Ghost is restoration. But, we must remember that God's conditions need to be met first. King David showed us what must be done. The Holy Ghost cannot move on our behalf if there is unconfessed sin in our lives. Once we repent of those sins, the hands of the Holy Ghost are untied, and He can move on our behalf.

(Read 2 Corinthians 3:17)

*****

AUGUST 3

Romans 7:23 (KJV) But I see another law in my members, warring against the law of my mind, and bringing me into captivity to the law of sin which is in my members.

The Law of sin and death wants to use our physical bodies as an implement of unrighteousness. It is constantly warring against our mind. It wants to bring us back into captivity to Satan. This will take control of us, if we do not keep our faith in Jesus and Him crucified. He has promised to keep us, as long as we keep our faith where it belongs.

(Read Galatians 5:17)

*****

AUGUST 4

Jeremiah 17:9 (KJV) The heart *is* deceitful above all *things*, and desperately wicked: who can know it?

God is the creator. He knows how corrupt the human heart is. One day Jesus spoke to a man named Nicodemus. He told this man that his birthright would not get him to Heaven. Jesus told him his good works would not get Him to Heaven. It takes a new birth, a total change of heart. It takes repentance from our sins and accepting Jesus Christ as Saviour. God then gives us a brand new heart. We are no longer the same person.

(Read Hebrews 3:15)

*****

AUGUST 5

Psalms 38:20-21 (KJV) (20) They also that render evil for good are mine adversaries; because I follow *the thing that* good *is*. (21) Forsake me not, O LORD: O my God, be not far from me.

We are reminded those who are evil are the enemies of God. This does not mean that God loves them less, it simple means they have chosen the pathway to Hell. That is an individual choice, and God has no control over it. But on the other hand, God is not far from those who serve Him.

(Read Psalm 35:22)

AUGUST 6

Hebrews 13:13 (KJV) Let us go forth therefore unto him without the camp, bearing his reproach.

Jesus Christ is the only bearer of salvation, He is the only door. As Christians, we share His rejection. As the world hates Him, it hates us also.

(Read Philippians 3:20)

*****

AUGUST 7

Psalms 138:7 (KJV) Though I walk in the midst of trouble, thou wilt revive me: thou shalt stretch forth thine hand against the wrath of mine enemies, and thy right hand shall save me.

Even when we stray, God is with us. He is always there to help us, especially when the enemy comes against us. He will deliver us with His strong right arm.

(Read Psalm 23:4)

*****

AUGUST 8

Job 1:21 (KJV) And said, Naked came I out of my mother's womb, and naked shall I return thither: the LORD gave, and the LORD hath taken away; blessed be the name of the LORD.

Job stayed faithful to the Lord regardless of what happened to him. He knew God was his deliverer. Job was and is an example to us. As Job remained a testimony to God, so can we, as long as we keep our faith in Jesus and Him crucified.

(Read James 1:17)

*****

AUGUST 9

Psalms 119:136 (KJV) Rivers of waters run down mine eyes, because they keep not thy law.

This verse is the thoughts of the Messiah. Jesus loves everyone, and He died for everyone. However, everyone does not choose to serve Him. This breaks the heart of Jesus, for He knows the destiny of those who will not serve Him. We should have the same thoughts concerning the lost and undone.

(Read Psalm 119:97)

*****

AUGUST 10

Matthew 7:13-14 (KJV) (13) Enter ye in at the strait gate: for wide *is* the gate, and broad *is* the way, that leadeth to destruction, and many there be which go in thereat: (14) Because strait *is* the gate, and narrow *is* the way, which leadeth unto life, and few there be that find it.

The strait gate is Jesus. Not only is the gate straight, but it is narrow also. There is no room to deviate from the course God has set for us. There are many religions in the world that claim to be the way to Heaven, but they are all false ways that will direct a person away from God, in place of to Him.

(Read Luke 13:24)

*****

AUGUST 11

Hebrews 11:24-25 (KJV) (24) By faith Moses, when he was come to years, refused to be called the son of Pharaoh's daughter; (25) Choosing rather to suffer affliction with the people of God, than to enjoy the pleasures of sin for a season;

When Moses "came to years", he was 40 years old. At that time, He chose to follow the God of his people, instead of being the Pharaoh of Egypt. He chose the things of God, rather than the things of this world. Sin always has a temporary pleasure, but the promises of God have eternal pleasure.

(Read Psalm 84:10)

*****

AUGUST 12

Habakkuk 3:17-18 (KJV) 17) Although the fig tree shall not blossom, neither *shall* fruit *be* in the vines; the labour of the olive shall fail, and the fields shall yield no meat; the flock shall be cut off from the fold, and *there shall be* no herd in the stalls: (18) Yet I will rejoice in the LORD, I will joy in the God of my salvation.

Though everything goes wrong, it does not matter. We can lose our job, and it will not matter. We may not be able to buy what we want to eat, and it will not matter. The fact is, the only thing that does matter is our relationship with God. If we keep our faith in Jesus and Him crucified, then God will provide everything else.

(Read Joel 2:23)

*****

AUGUST 13

Psalms 119:50 (KJV) This *is* my comfort in my affliction: for thy word hath quickened me.

Jesus does not say we will not suffer affliction. He does not even guarantee that He will provide us with a way around affliction. What He does promise is He will be with us even when we are in affliction.

(Read Romans 15:4)

*****

AUGUST 14

1 Peter 2:21 (KJV) For even hereunto were ye called: because Christ also suffered for us, leaving us an example, that ye should follow his steps.

As children of God, we are called to act Christ like. We cannot forget that Jesus suffered for us. He suffered in our place. It is our calling to live the Christ life before others, that they might see Jesus in us. The Holy Ghost will lead, guide, and direct us in this, as long as we allow Him to.

(Read Matthew 11:29)

*****

AUGUST 15

Hebrews 12:1 (KJV) Wherefore seeing we also are compassed about with so great a cloud of witnesses, let us lay aside every weight, and the sin which doth so easily beset *us*, and let us run with patience the race that is set before us,

This verse is referring to the Old Testament saints, as well as the New Testament saints. God has provided us with a vast number of witnesses about Himself, and what He did at Calvary. This should be enough to encourage us in our Christian walk.

(Read 2 Corinthians 7:1)

*****

AUGUST 16

James 5:10 (KJV) Take, my brethren, the prophets, who have spoken in the name of the Lord, for an example of suffering affliction, and of patience.

Even the prophets of old were not exempt from affliction. They spoke in the name of the Lord, yet they were an example of suffering, affliction, and patience. Are you an example the Lord can use? Perhaps there is a weaker Christian out there watching how you go through the afflictions you face. Are they getting stronger or weaker as they observe you?

(Read 2 Peter 1:21)

*****

AUGUST 17

Jeremiah 31:19 (KJV) Surely after that I was turned, I repented; and after that I was instructed, I smote upon *my* thigh: I was ashamed, yea, even confounded, because I did bear the reproach of my youth.

It takes a desire to turn from your sinful ways in order to truly repent. But, you cannot change your ways before you repent. You do not have the strength in yourself to do that. Once you have repented and turned to God, then God gives you His strength. That is the strength needed to turn your life around.

(Read Deuteronomy 30:2-3)

*****

AUGUST 18

Hosea 5:15 (KJV) I will go *and* return to my place, till they acknowledge their offence, and seek my face: in their affliction they will seek me early.

This is the thoughts of God, as He sees people who stop serving Him. He steps back away from them, until they see where they are actually at, and turn back to Him. When thy have done that, then God will deliver them from affliction.

(Read Psalm 63:1)

*****

AUGUST 19

James 1:3-4 (KJV) (3) Knowing *this*, that the trying of your faith worketh patience. (4) But let patience have *her* perfect work, that ye may be perfect and entire, wanting nothing.

If we have genuine faith, testing will come our way. This develops and strengthens the faith we have. We should not be discouraged when testing comes our way. God is working to make you mature and complete in Him.

(Read 1 Peter 1:7)

*****

AUGUST 20

Job 10:15 (KJV) If I be wicked, woe unto me; and *if* I be righteous, *yet* will I not lift up my head. *I am* full of confusion; therefore see thou mine affliction;

Job is confused about what He is going through, but God does not hold this against Him. God did not give Job any explanation about why He allowed all of the testing Job went through, so he simple did not understand. Sometimes we are confused by the testing God allows us to go through. This is not a bad thing. Just remember, in God's timing, He will deliver you, just as He did Job.

(Read Psalm 3:3)

*****

AUGUST 21

Psalms 39:9 (KJV) I was dumb, I opened not my mouth; because thou didst *it*.

This is actually prophecy concerning the trial of Jesus. He was not to defend Himself, for it was the will of God for Him not to answer His accusers. He sacrificed Himself, in your place. He did it, to restore your relationship with God. It is up to you to make sure Jesus did not sacrifice Himself in vain.

(Read Psalm 49:15)

*****

AUGUST 22

Psalms 42:5 (KJV) Why art thou cast down, O my soul? And *why* art thou disquieted in me? hope thou in God: for I shall yet praise him *for* the help of his countenance.

David questioned his faith in God. In doing so, he reminded himself that all victory comes through God, and then David began to rejoice. Take a look at your relationship with God. Remind yourself that God has the victory for you also. Then, begin to rejoice, just like David did.

(Read Lamentations 3:24)

*****

AUGUST 23

Hebrews 12:11 (KJV) Now no chastening for the present seemeth to be joyous, but grievous: nevertheless afterward it yieldeth the peaceable fruit of righteousness unto them which are exercised thereby.

Trials are never pleasant to go through. Sometimes, they are certainly very hard to bear. After the trial is over, we find we have grown in the Lord. Let us not forget this the next time we find ourselves in the midst of a trial.

(Read 1 Thessalonians 5:18)

*****

AUGUST 24

Job 23:10 (KJV) But he knoweth the way that I take: *when* **he hath tried me, I shall come forth as gold.**

What a wonderful statement Job makes here. God always knows where we are at. He always knows what we are going through. Nothing gets past Him. When all is said and done, God will see that we come forth as gold. He always brings the victory!

(Read James 1:12)

*****

AUGUST 25

Job 36:8-9 (KJV) (8) And if *they be* **bound in fetters,** *and* **be holden in cords of affliction; (9) Then he showeth them their work, and their transgressions that they have exceeded.**

Oh the convicting power of the Holy Ghost. We He begins to

convict of sin, then a person begins to see themselves as God sees them. They begin to see just how wicked they are. When this happens, a person must either run to the altar, or run the other direction, away from God.

(Read Psalm 107:10-11)

*****

AUGUST 26

Psalms 79:8 (KJV) O remember not against us former iniquities: let thy tender mercies speedily prevent us: for we are brought very low.

True repentance is more than saying a few words. First of all, it is realizing that we are totally separated from God because of our sins. Secondly, asking forgiveness for those sins, and never wanting to do them again. Thirdly, it is asking Jesus to forgive those sins you never want to do again, and asking Him to come into your life, to lead, guide, and direct you.

(Read Isaiah 64:9)

*****

AUGUST 27

Hosea 2:6-7 (KJV) (6) Therefore, behold, I will hedge up thy way with thorns, and make a wall, that she shall not find her paths. (7) And she shall follow after her lovers, but she shall not overtake them; and she shall seek them,

but shall not find *them*: **then shall she say, I will go and return to my first husband; for then** *was it* **better with me than now.**

Gomer was determined to follow her evil ways. God was determined to stop her, and turn her life around. God could not force His will upon her, but He could change circumstances to the point her desire would be to change. Are you listening to God's desires for your life? Are you like Gomer, and determined to do your own thing? Don't be surprised if circumstances in your life begin to change,

(Read Luke 15:17-18)

*****

AUGUST 28

1 Peter 1:6-7 (KJV) (6) Wherein ye greatly rejoice, though now for a season, if need be, ye are in heaviness through manifold temptations: (7) That the trial of your faith, being much more precious than of gold that perisheth, though it be tried with fire, might be found unto praise and honour and glory at the appearing of Jesus Christ:

There is coming a time when life as we know it will be over. The last trump will sound, and we will be changed. Until that time, we must face many things, for our faith must be tested. It must be tested to see if it is genuine. God already knows whether it is or not, so the testing is for your benefit. You need to see whether your faith is true or not. This makes it more precious than gold. We are currently be prepared and made ready for the rapture.

(Read 1 Corinthians 1:7)

*****

AUGUST 29

Isaiah 38:12 (KJV) Mine age is departed, and is removed from me as a shepherd's tent: I have cut off like a weaver my life: he will cut me off with pining sickness: from day *even* to night wilt thou make an end of me.

It seems that Isaiah is not actually afraid he will die. He has much work for God that he feels he still needs to do. As such, Isaiah's concern is that he will be taken out before his work is complete. What about you? Do you still have work for God that still needs to be completed? Are you busy trying to get it finished?

(Read 2 Corinthians 5:1)

*****

AUGUST 30

2 Corinthians 1:9-10 (KJV) (9) But we had the sentence of death in ourselves, that we should not trust in ourselves, but in God which raiseth the dead: (10) Who delivered us from so great a death, and doth deliver: in whom we trust that he will yet deliver *us*;

We were once in sin, and because of that, we had a death sentence. This is referring to the second death, which is eternal torment. As Christians, we must not put any confidence in ourselves to affect our eternity, for we have no control over it. Our confidence must be in god, for He alone has power over everything. Once our work on this earth is finished, the Lord will transport us into eternal life. Let's trust Him.

(Read 2 Timothy 3:11)

*****

AUGUST 31

2 Corinthians 4:17 (KJV) For our light affliction, which is but for a moment, worketh for us a far more exceeding *and* eternal weight of glory;

When we consider the reward God has for us, then even the worst afflictions we face seem light. When compared to eternity, the length of any affliction is short. Our final reward will be received at the resurrection.

(Read 1 Corinthians 12:31)

*****

SEPTEMBER 1

Job 1:12 (KJV) And the LORD said unto Satan, Behold, all that he hath *is* in thy power; only upon himself put not forth thine hand. So Satan went forth from the presence of the LORD.

Although Satan was allowed to attack Job, limitations were placed on him. Let us not forget, when Satan comes against us, he has limited authority. God is the one who is in complete control. Satan will try to convince you otherwise. When he does, remember the story of Job.

(Read Job 1:5)

*****

SEPTEMBER 2

James 1:13-14 (KJV) (13) Let no man say when he is tempted, I am tempted of God: for God cannot be tempted with evil, neither tempteth he any man: (14) But every man is tempted, when he is drawn away of his own lust, and enticed.

Never think when you are tempted to sin, that the temptation comes from God. God does not tempt man to sin. All temptation comes from Satan.

(Read 1 John 1:5)

*****

SEPTEMBER 3

2 Corinthians 2:11 (KJV) Lest Satan should get an advantage of us: for we are not ignorant of his devices.

Let us remember, as long as we obey the Word of God, Satan does not have the ability to overcome us. Also, as Christians who know and understand the Word of God, we are aware of the devices Satan tries to use against us. He cannot lead us in the wrong direction, unless we allow him to.

(Read 1 Thessalonians 4:7)

*****

SEPTEMBER 4

Romans 7:21 (KJV) I find then a law, that, when I would do good, evil is present with me.

This is referring to the "Law of sin and death", not the Law of Moses. The "sin nature" is always with the believer. Every time we try to do what is good, the sin nature tries to cause us to do just the opposite. The only way to overcome the sin nature, is to keep our faith in Jesus and Him crucified.

(Read 1 Corinthians 15:57)

*****

SEPTEMBER 5

1 Timothy 6:9 (KJV) But they that will be rich fall into temptation and a snare, and *into* many foolish and hurtful lusts, which drown men in destruction and perdition.

They that are rich face temptations many of us cannot fathom. The greatest of these is the temptation to sacrifice principles. These temptations can lead to the wreck and ruin of both mind and body, which can include the loss of their eternal soul. Just remember, unless we keep our faith in Jesus and Him crucified, any of us can fall to temptation.

(Read Matthew 19:23)

*****

SEPTEMBER 6

Proverbs 29:25 (KJV) The fear of man bringeth a snare: but whoso putteth his trust in the LORD shall be safe.

You can either fear man or fear God. You cannot fear both. If you fear man, you will become a slave to the man. Safety is only guaranteed to those who fear and serve the Lord, and put complete trust in Him.

(Read Psalm 25:2)

*****

SEPTEMBER 7

Galatians 5:7 (KJV) Ye did run well; who did hinder you that ye should not obey the truth?

The Galatians went astray, because they had started listening to false teachers. We have many false teachers today, who are trying to get your eyes off Jesus and the cross. Keep your faith where it belongs, and do not follow the false teachers.

(Read Galatians 3:1)

*****

SEPTEMBER 8

Galatians 3:3 (KJV) Are ye so foolish? having begun in the Spirit, are ye now made perfect by the flesh?

Do you think you can come to spiritual maturity by your own self efforts? The Galatians were practicing salvation by faith, and sanctification by self. This does not work. Many today are attempting the same thing. Just as it did not work for the Galatians, it will not work for those today either, for God still will not accept it. Sanctification can only come about by keeping your faith in Jesus and Him crucified,

(Read Galatians 4:9)

*****

SEPTEMBER 9

Romans 3:2 (KJV) Much every way: chiefly, because that unto them were committed the oracles of God.

The Word of God was originally given to the Jews, in order to share with the world. But, these words and laws could only serve as a school master, until the Lord Jesus Christ came. All the sacrifices of the Law pointed to Jesus. He is the Way, the Truth, and the Life. Only faith in Him and His sacrifice at Calvary can bring us salvation and sanctification.

(Read 1 Peter 4:11)

*****

SEPTEMBER 10

Revelation 2:4-5 (KJV) (4) Nevertheless I have *somewhat* against thee, because thou hast left thy first love. (5) Remember therefore from whence thou art fallen, and repent, and do the first works; or else I will come unto thee quickly, and will remove thy candlestick out of his place, except thou repent.

Jesus is speaking to a church in this Scripture. Remember, a church is not a building, it is the people within the building. Jesus says He has something against them, for they have left their first love. This means they stopped following Jesus and the cross. They had actually turned their backs on God and stopped serving Him, while still attending church. He tells them the need to repent and do their first works over. Remember this, and never take your faith off of Jesus and Him crucified.

(Read Revelation 2:11)

*****

SEPTEMBER 11

1 Corinthians 9:27 (KJV) But I keep under my body, and bring *it* into subjection: lest that by any means, when I have preached to others, I myself should be a castaway.

Paul understood that all victory comes through the cross of Calvary. He knew if he did not keep his faith on the sacrifice Jesus made, then he was subject to fall. The Lord only has one way to victory. It does not matter if you are a preacher, or a layman, only Jesus and Him crucified brings complete and total victory.

(Read 2 Corinthians 4:5)

*****

SEPTEMBER 12

Romans 6:1 (KJV) What shall we say then? Shall we continue in sin, that grace may abound?

This is a good question. The answer is no. Grace does not provide a license to sin. It provides the strength to overcome sin through Jesus and the cross of Calvary.

(Read Romans 5:21)

*****

SEPTEMBER 13

1 Corinthians 4:7(KJV) For who maketh thee to differ *from another*? and what hast thou that thou didst not receive? now if thou didst receive *it*, why dost thou glory, as if thou hadst not received *it*?

Everyone starts on the same level. Everyone starts out in desperate need of God. Once we are saved, it does not mean you deserve it. Salvation is a Gift of God. This gift is provided because of the sacrifice Jesus made on the cross.

(Read James 1:18)

*****

SEPTEMBER 14

Psalms 73:2-3 (KJV) (2) But as for me, my feet were almost gone; my steps had well nigh slipped. (3) For I was envious at the foolish, *when* I saw the prosperity of the wicked.

Asaph the writer of this Psalm was preoccupied with self. Self always causes us to take our eyes off of Jesus. Self can only be conquered when we hide ourselves in Jesus Christ.

(Read John 14:20)

*****

SEPTEMBER 15

Matthew 6:30 (KJV) Wherefore, if God so clothe the grass of the field, which to day is, and to morrow is cast into the oven, *shall he* not much more *clothe* you, O ye of little faith?

God carefully takes care of the grass of the field. How much more is he willing to help you and take care of you? He really does care for you. That is why Jesus went to Calvary in your place.

(Read Luke 12:29-30)

SEPTEMBER 16

Psalms 69:2-3(KJV) (2) I sink in deep mire, where *there is* no standing: I am come into deep waters, where the floods overflow me. (3) I am weary of my crying: my throat is dried: mine eyes fail while I wait for my God.

This is how David felt after his sin with Bathsheba. In reading these words, we can understand the horror of sin. He realized the place he was in. He was separated from God. Still yet, David realized the need to call upon God. When we stumble, and when we fall, we need to realize as David did, that it is time to call upon God. He still hears, and still forgives, if we ask Him to.

(Read Psalm 31:24)

*****

SEPTEMBER 17

2 Corinthians 12:7 (KJV) And lest I should be exalted above measure through the abundance of the revelations, there was given to me a thorn in the flesh, the messenger of Satan to buffet me, lest I should be exalted above measure.

Paul was under constant attack from Satan. He knew the cause of these attacks was his knowledge of the great revelation God had given him concerning the message of Jesus and Him crucified. Paul was not complaining about it though. He understood God as allowing this to take place so he would not get exalted in himself. Like Paul, sometimes God allows things to happen to us for our benefit. Remember, God knows what is best for us.

(Read Job 2:6-7)

*****

SEPTEMBER 18

Ephesians 6:12 (KJV) For we wrestle not against flesh and blood, but against principalities, against powers, against the rulers of the darkness of this world, against spiritual wickedness in high *places*.

We need to realize as Christians, our enemies are not human. Satan does use humans to come against us, but he is the one pulling the strings. Principalities are spiritual beings of the highest rank and order in Satan's kingdom. Powers is the rank of spiritual beings just below the "Principalities. The rulers of darkness of this world are the spirit beings who carry out the instructions of the "Powers". Finally, the spiritual wickedness in high place refers to the demon spirits. Although Satan has an active force working against us, God is still the all-powerful one, and we are under His protection, as long as we keep our faith in Jesus and Him crucified.

(Read 1 Corinthians 9:25)

*****

SEPTEMBER 19

Proverbs 4:14-15(KJV) (14) Enter not into the path of the wicked, and go not in the way of evil *men*. (15) Avoid it, pass not by it, turn from it, and pass away.

We know from the Word of God, "the path of the wicked" is constantly calling us. In these verses, the Holy Ghost is giving us a fourfold warning. He warns us to avoid it, pass not by it, to turn from it, and to pass away from it. We are not able to overcome all this in our own strength. It takes keeping our faith in the Lord Jesus Christ and His sacrifice at Calvary. When we do, then we are able to stand in His strength.

(Read Psalm 1:1)

*****

SEPTEMBER 20

Matthew 26:41 (KJV) Watch and pray, that ye enter not into temptation: the spirit indeed *is* willing, but the flesh *is* weak.

We are warned here, that anyone can enter into temptation. This is temptation to turn against the Lord, and to stop serving Him. The spirit of man is willing to serve the Lord, but the flesh is weak, it does not have the strength to stand on its own. These battles can only be won by our faith being placed completely in Jesus and His crucifixion. This then gives the Holy Ghost the ability to work in our lives.

(Read Galatians 5:17)

*****

SEPTEMBER 21

Ephesians 6:16 (KJV) Above all, taking the shield of faith, wherewith ye shall be able to quench all the fiery darts of the wicked.

If we are taking up the Shield of Faith, then we are keeping our faith on Jesus and Him crucified. This is the only faith that God recognizes. It is also the only faith Satan recognizes. Fiery darts represents the temptations Satan attacks us with. But, when we are using the Shield of Faith, it will stop all the fiery darts of the Devil.

(Read 1 John 5:4)

*****

SEPTEMBER 22

Ephesians 6:13 (KJV) Wherefore take unto you the whole armour of God, that ye may be able to withstand in the evil day, and having done all, to stand.

We need the Armor of God because of what we face each and every day. This gives us the ability to resist and overcome the power of the enemy. "To stand" refers to not giving any ground at all to the enemy. We are wearing the "Armor of God" as long as we keep our faith in Jesus and Him crucified.

(Read Ephesians 1:3)

*****

SEPTEMBER 23

Revelation 3:10 (KJV) Because thou hast kept the word of my patience, I also will keep thee from the hour of temptation, which shall come upon all the world, to try them that dwell upon the earth.

The hour of temptation is the period of the Great Tribulation. God is telling us here, that the church will be kept from the Great Tribulation. This notifies us that the Rapture will take place before the Great Tribulation period.

(Read 2 Peter 2:9)

*****

SEPTEMBER 24

James 1:12 (KJV) Blessed *is* the man that endureth temptation: for when he is tried, he shall receive the crown of life, which the Lord hath promised to them that love him.

Temptation is a test of faith. James says when we endure such temptation, that we will receive the Crown of Life. This is a reward much greater than the price paid. If we really love the Lord, we will keep His commandments. We can accomplish this with the help of the Holy Ghost. This requires us to keep our faith in Jesus and Him crucified.

(Read 1 Peter 3:14-16)

*****

SEPTEMBER 25

2 Peter 2:9 (KJV) The Lord knoweth how to deliver the godly out of temptations, and to reserve the unjust unto the day of judgment to be punished:

We are delivered "out of temptations" by placing and keeping our faith in Jesus and His sacrifice on the cross. This gives the Holy Ghost the authority to deliver us. Peter also tells us that everyone who rejects Jesus and His sacrifice will be judged.

(Read 1 Corinthians 10:13)

*****

SEPTEMBER 26

2 Corinthians 12:9 (KJV) And he said unto me, My grace is sufficient for thee: for my strength is made perfect in weakness. Most gladly therefore will I rather glory in my infirmities, that the power of Christ may rest upon me.

Although this was spoken to the Apostle Paul, it is a reminder to us today also. The Grace of the Lord is sufficient for us. Actually, that is all we need. We need to realize that we cannot stand in our own strength, for that is our weakness.

Satan will defeat us every time we try to defeat him in our own strength. But, when we lean on Jesus, by putting our faith on Him and His crucifixion, then the strength of the Holy Ghost is made perfect in us. We can then glory in our weakness, for we know we are resting in Jesus, and He wins the battle for us each and every time.

(Read Philippians 4:13)

*****

SEPTEMBER 27

Hebrews 2:18 (KJV) For in that he himself hath suffered being tempted, he is able to succour them that are tempted.

As a man upon this earth, Jesus was tempted to sin. He overcame that temptation, and was the only perfect man. Because of this, He understands what we as humans go through. We can also overcome temptation, but not in our own ability. We can overcome temptation by placing our faith in Jesus and His crucifixion. This is the only way temptation can be overcome, for this gives the Holy Ghost the ability to strengthen us.

(Read Hebrews 4:15)

*****

SEPTEMBER 28

Luke 22:31-32 (KJV) (31) And the Lord said, Simon, Simon, behold, Satan hath desired *to have* you, that he may sift *you* as wheat: (32) But I have prayed for thee, that thy faith fail not: and when thou art converted, strengthen thy brethren.

These verses give us a glimpse into the spirit world. As Satan tempted Job, he also wanted to tempt Peter. Satan tempts us, to bring out the bad in us. God tests us, to bring out the good in us. Satan attacks always comes against our faith. He wants us to give up, and stop serving the Lord. God wants us to come to the right path of trust and dependence on Him, instead of on self.

(Read 1 Peter 5:8)

*****

SEPTEMBER 29

Matthew 6:13 (KJV) And lead us not into temptation, but deliver us from evil: For thine is the kingdom, and the power, and the glory, for ever. Amen.

This is a plea for help. Do not let me be tempted because of my own self-confidence. Self-confidence comes from the flesh, and not from the Spirit of God. Only God can deliver from temptation. He delivers by the power of the Holy Ghost, according to our faith in Jesus and Him crucified. God delivers, and all glory belongs to Him.

(Read 1 Chronicles 29:11)

*****

SEPTEMBER 30

Romans 3:21 (KJV) But now the righteousness of God without the law is manifested, being witnessed by the law and the prophets;

The Law of Moses shows us the righteousness of God. It clearly spells out that the penalty for sin is death. It even spells out the Divine Principle of Justification by faith. The law however could not provide justification. The Law only brings death, but God brings life through Jesus Christ.

(Read Philippians 3:9)

*****

CHAPTER 10 - OCTOBER

OCTOBER 1

Deuteronomy 8:2 (KJV) And thou shalt remember all the way which the LORD thy God led thee these forty years in the wilderness, to humble thee, *and* to prove thee, to know what *was* in thine heart, whether thou wouldest keep his commandments, or no.

With the believer, everything is a test. Look back at your Christian life. Look at the good things, and look at the bad things. Then you can begin to realize where God has moved on your behalf. Take time now to thank Him for what He has done for you.

(Read Deuteronomy 5:33)

*****

OCTOBER 2

1 Samuel 7:12 (KJV) Then Samuel took a stone, and set *it* between Mizpeh and Shen, and called the name of it Ebenezer, saying, Hitherto hath the LORD helped us.

The stone Samuel picked up and used represented Jesus Christ. Samuel went on to say, "Hitherto hath the Lord helped us". This verse is letting us know the Lord will always help us, as long as we keep our faith in Jesus and Him crucified.

(Read Joshua 24:26-27)

*****

OCTOBER 3

2 Samuel 7:18-19 (KJV) (18) Then went king David in, and sat before the LORD, and he said, Who *am* I, O Lord GOD? and what *is* my house, that thou hast brought me hitherto? (19) And this was yet a small thing in thy sight, O Lord GOD; but thou hast spoken also of thy servant's house for a great while to come. And *is* this the manner of man, O Lord GOD?

David was overwhelmed by all that was happening. He was just beginning to understand that God's thoughts are always much bigger than ours. Somehow through all this, David understood the Messiah was coming from his house. Even then God was making manifest a plan to redeem man.

(Read Isaiah 55:8)

OCTOBER 4

Psalms 119:65 (KJV) Thou hast dealt well with thy servant, O LORD, according unto thy word.

Staying true to God's Word guarantees His blessings. God always honors His Word, and nothing else. He is so faithful!

(Read Psalm 119:169-170)

*****

OCTOBER 5

Lamentations 3:22-23 (KJV) (22) *It is of* the LORD'S mercies that we are not consumed, because his compassions fail not. (23) *They are* new every morning: great *is* thy faithfulness.

God is faithful. Even when it looks like the enemy is going to destroy us, He is there to rescue us. We need to remember that God's mercy cannot be exhausted. Jeremiah says God's mercy renews every morning. This will never change as long as we keep our faith in Jesus and Him crucified. Jeremiah said it all, when he said, "Great is Thy faithfulness."

(Read Malachi 3:6)

*****

OCTOBER 6

Psalms 103:10 (KJV) He hath not dealt with us after our sins; nor rewarded us according to our iniquities.

God is not quick to deal with us about our sins. If He so desired, He could punish us at any moment, but He does not do that. He prefers us to come to the knowledge about ours sins, and approach Him for forgiveness.

(Read Ezra 9:13)

*****

OCTOBER 7

Psalms 16:7 (KJV) I will bless the LORD, who hath given me counsel: my reins also instruct me in the night seasons.

It should be our goal to bless the Lord. He has done so much for us. He leads us, and guides us. He even instructs us in His ways, as well as protects us. He is so worthy of our praise.

(Read Psalm 17:3)

*****

OCTOBER 8

Joshua 23:14 (KJV) And, behold, this day I *am* going the way of all the earth: and ye know in all your hearts and in all your souls, that not one thing hath failed of all the good things which the LORD your God spake concerning you; all are come to pass unto you, *and* not one thing hath failed thereof.

Unless the Rapture takes place first, then we will all face death as Joshua did. But, like Joshua, we can declare that God has never failed us. Everything He has promised has come to pass, or will come to pass. Let us not forget, that God will never fail us.

(Read Joshua 21:45)

*****

OCTOBER 9

Psalms 40:5 (KJV) Many, O LORD my God, *are* thy wonderful works *which* thou hast done, and thy thoughts *which are* to us-ward: they cannot be reckoned up in order unto thee: *if* I would declare and speak *of them*, they are more than can be numbered.

Though many preachers try to deny it today, God's wonderful works are so many, that He can provide for every need. We could spend the rest of our lives proclaiming all that God has done, and still not scratch the surface. He is so good to us and deserves all of our praise.

(Read Psalm 9:1)

*****

OCTOBER 10

2 Timothy 3:14 (KJV) But continue thou in the things which thou hast learned and hast been assured of, knowing of whom thou hast learned *them*;

Timothy learned the Word of God from Paul, which includes the New Covenant. The New Covenant is all about what all Jesus accomplished at Calvary. The New Covenant was given directly to Paul from the Lord. Because of this, it had to be taught by Paul.

(Read 2 Timothy 1:13)

*****

OCTOBER 11

Colossians 1:21 (KJV) And you, that were sometime alienated and enemies in *your* mind by wicked works, yet now hath he reconciled us to Himself.

We were once separated from God, and we were His enemies, in our minds, and because of the wicked things we did. But, God has re-established us to Himself through the price Jesus paid on Calvary

(Read Ephesians 2:12-13)

OCTOBER 12

Job 13:23 (KJV) How many *are* mine iniquities and sins? make me to know my transgression and my sin.

Job's friends tried to tell him that he was a sinner, and at one time he was. Just like at one time we all were sinners. Then there was a time when we cried out to God with words similar to these. When we did, God not only heard them, He also washed us white as snow with the ***blood*** of Jesus.

(Read Psalm 19:12)

*****

OCTOBER 13

Romans 6:20-21 (KJV) (20) For when ye were the servants of sin, ye were free from righteousness. (21) What fruit had ye then in those things whereof ye are now ashamed? for the end of those things *is* death

We were once slaves to sin, and had nothing to do with righteousness. Absolutely nothing of value came from the life of sin that we lived. In fact, it is impossible to bear good fruit while living a life of sin. If we fail to keep our faith on Jesus and Him crucified, then the sin nature will eventually take over our lives, and spiritual death will be the conclusion. Let's keep our faith on Jesus and His sacrifice.

(Read Romans 6:22)

*****

OCTOBER 14

Colossians 1:12-13 (KJV) (12) Giving thanks unto the Father, which hath made us meet to be partakers of the inheritance of the saints in light: (13) Who hath delivered us from the power of darkness, and hath translated *us* into the kingdom of his dear Son:

We should constantly be giving thanks to our Heavenly Father. Thankfully, God has given us a part in the inheritance of the saints, because of our standing in Christ Jesus. Because of His battle on the cross, Jesus rescued us from the powers of darkness.

(Read 1 Thessalonians 1:10)

*****

OCTOBER 15

Psalms 86:13 (KJV) For great *is* thy mercy toward me: and thou hast delivered my soul from the lowest hell.

Thank God for His Mercy. Thank God for His Amazing Grace! This is actually a prophecy concerning Jesus Christ, but because of the sacrifice of Jesus, we can make the same declaration.

(Read Psalm 116:8)

OCTOBER 16

Song of Songs 2:3-4 (KJV)
(3) As the apple tree among the trees of the wood, so *is* my beloved among the sons. I sat down under his shadow with great delight, and his fruit *was* sweet to my taste. (4) He brought me to the banqueting house, and his banner over me *was* love.

From these verses, we see four things a Christian is given when Christ is accepted into one's life. 1. "I sat down": in union with Him, and there is rest, 2. "With great delight" there is joy. 3. "In His shadow: there is shelter from the heat. 4. "His fruit was sweet to my taste": in Christ there is plenty to sustain us. One day we will be brought to the great banquet, which is the marriage supper of the Lamb.

(Read Isaiah 25:4)

*****

OCTOBER 17

Psalms 119:92 (KJV) Unless thy law *had been* my delights, I should then have perished in mine affliction.

If it had not been for God's plan of salvation, then we would be on the road to a Devil's Hell. But, because we have put our faith in Jesus and what He did at Calvary, we shall be able to delight in the Lord now, and forever.

(Read Psalm 119:113)

OCTOBER 18

Psalms 116:1-2 (KJV) (1) I love the LORD, because he hath heard my voice *and* my supplications. (2) Because he hath inclined his ear unto me, therefore will I call upon *him* as long as I live.

Thank God, He has heard our voice. Thank God He knew our need, even before we were able to call out to Him. Because He did, we can now spend time in communion with God for the rest of our lives, and into eternity.

(Read Psalm 18:1-2)

*****

OCTOBER 19

Psalms 31:7 (KJV) I will be glad and rejoice in thy mercy: for thou hast considered my trouble; thou hast known my soul in adversities;

God is always concerned about the trouble we face. He wants us to call upon Him in our time of need. He knows our needs and our adversities. We can always be glad and rejoice in God's mercy.

(Read Psalm 37:18)

*****

OCTOBER 20

Lamentations 3:57-58 (KJV) (57) Thou drewest near in the day *that* I called upon thee: thou saidst, Fear not. (58) O Lord, thou hast pleaded the causes of my soul; thou hast redeemed my life.

The words "Fear not" are given to every true Christian. That is because God is always drawing near to us when we call upon Him. Thank God, at Calvary, He pleaded the causes of our souls, and redeemed our lives.

(Read James 4:8)

*****

OCTOBER 21

Psalms 30:3 (KJV) O LORD, thou hast brought up my soul from the grave: thou hast kept me alive, that I should not go down to the pit.

We were headed for the grave. To go a step farther, we were headed toward the second death, which is eternal torment. But, God raised Jesus up victorious over death, Hell, and the grave. As children of God, He has delivered us, and provided us with eternal life.

(Read Psalm 86:13)

*****

OCTOBER 22

Genesis 47:9 (KJV) And Jacob said unto Pharaoh, The days of the years of my pilgrimage *are* an hundred and thirty years: few and evil have the days of the years of my life been, and have not attained unto the days of the years of the life of my fathers in the days of their pilgrimage.

The life of Jacob was not as long as those of his family who lived before him. But, Jacob ended up living a tremendous life for God. We are the same, some live longer than others, some do not. What counts is what we are able to accomplish for God during the lifespan we have. Let us be sure to redeem the time.

(Read Hebrews 11:9-10)

*****

OCTOBER 23

1 Thessalonians 4:13-14 (KJV) (13) But I would not have you to be ignorant, brethren, concerning them which are asleep, that ye sorrow not, even as others which have no hope. (14) For if we believe that Jesus died and rose again, even so them also which sleep in Jesus will God bring with him.

Paul is referring to believers who have died. We are not to sorrow for each other the same way the world does. We have hope they do not have, for they have no hope at all. We are looking for the first resurrection, and eternal life. At death, the soul and spirit of the child of God goes back to God instantly, while the body returns to dust. At the rapture, God will replace the physical body with a glorified body. He will then unite that glorified body with the soul and spirit, thus making the believer whole.

(Read 1 Thessalonians 3:13)

*****

OCTOBER 24

Psalms 71:17-18 (KJV) (17) O God, thou hast taught me from my youth: and hitherto have I declared thy wondrous works. (18) Now also when I am old and greyheaded, O God, forsake me not; until I have showed thy strength unto *this* generation, *and* thy power to every one *that* is to come.

These should be our thoughts as well, praising God for all He has done. He has kept us through our youth, and we should be thankful for that. Now, we need to be concerned with the rest of our lives. What does God want us to do, and how much time do we have to do it. We must work while it is yet day, meaning while we still have time to do it.

(Read Psalm 36:5)

*****

OCTOBER 25

Psalms 116:12-13 (KJV) (12) What shall I render unto the LORD *for* all his benefits toward me? (13) I will take the cup of salvation, and call upon the name of the LORD.

We cannot render (give) anything to God for what He has done for us. God has nothing for sale, it is all a free gift, because of God's Grace. As children of God, He has given us the right to not only make requests to our Heavenly Father, but to also expect an answer.

(Read Psalm 16:5)

*****

OCTOBER 26

Psalms 77:5-6 (KJV) (5) I have considered the days of old, the years of ancient times. (6) I call to remembrance my song in the night: I commune with mine own heart: and my spirit made diligent search.

Sometimes we need to look back. It could be so we can see how far we have come. Sometimes it could be to examine how far we have strayed. Either way, we should also check to see where God desires for us to be. We can then take the necessary steps to reach the goal God has for us.

(Read Psalm 4:4)

*****

OCTOBER 27

Genesis 32:10 (KJV) I am not worthy of the least of all the mercies, and of all the truth, which thou hast showed unto thy servant; for with my staff I passed over this Jordan; and now I am become two bands.

This prayer of Jacob is the first prayer recorded in the Bible. Like Jacob, we are not worthy of the least of all God's mercies. We also cannot do anything without God. What we do have, is provided to us because of what Jesus did at Calvary, not anything we have done.

(Read Genesis 28:13–15)

*****

OCTOBER 28

Job 34:31-32 (KJV) (31) Surely it is meet to be said unto God, I have borne *chastisement*, I will not offend *any more*: (32) *That which* I see not teach thou me: if I have done iniquity, I will do no more.

This would make a beautiful prayer. I have gone through my chastisement, and I have learned my lesson. I will not sin anymore. Teach me your ways, and I will not sin any longer. This is the attitude of heart God desires us to have.

(Read Psalm 19:12)

*****

OCTOBER 29

Psalms 119:59-60 (KJV) (59) I thought on my ways, and turned my feet unto thy testimonies. (60) I made haste, and delayed not to keep thy commandments.

God wants us to turn to His Word. He wants us to read His Word. He wants us to study His Word. He wants us to know His Word. Only by knowing God's Word will we be able to live the life for God He wants us to live.

(Read Acts 16:25)

*****

OCTOBER 30

Psalms 116:7-8 (KJV) (7) Return unto thy rest, O my soul; for the LORD hath dealt bountifully with thee. (8) For thou hast delivered my soul from death, mine eyes from tears, *and* my feet from falling.

Jesus is our Sabbath. This means He is our rest. Jesus has provided everything for us through His sacrifice on Calvary. Because of that, we can have complete trust in Him, and rest completely in Him. He has delivered us from eternal torment, one day, in the near future, He will wipe away all of our tears.

(Read Jeremiah 6:16)

*****

OCTOBER 31

1 Samuel 12:24 (KJV) Only fear the LORD, and serve him in truth with all your heart: for consider how great *things* he hath done for you.

We are to serve the Lord with our whole heart, our whole mind, and our whole soul. Jesus is Truth, for He has done all things for us. On a daily basis, we should stop and think about all the great things He has done.

(Read 1 Samuel 12:14).

*****

NOVEMBER 1

Psalms 31:15-16 (KJV) (15) My times *are* in thy hand: deliver me from the hand of mine enemies, and from them that persecute me. (16) Make thy face to shine upon thy servant: save me for thy mercies' sake.

Our lives and our mission for the Lord are in God's hands, not the hands of Satan, or the hands of man. The Face of the Lord shines on His children, and he takes care of them.

(Read Numbers 6:25-26)

*****

NOVEMBER 2

Psalms 37:3-4 (KJV) (3) Trust in the LORD, and do good; *so* shalt thou dwell in the land, and verily thou shalt be fed. (4) Delight thyself also in the LORD; and he shall give thee the desires of thine heart.

We should not look to the world or at the world. We should always look at the Lord, and put all of our trust in Him. Also, we should take great pleasure in serving the Lord. When we do, He will give us the desires of our heart.

(Read Job 22:26)

*****

NOVEMBER 3

Psalms 71:20 (KJV) *Thou*, which hast showed me great and sore troubles, shalt quicken me again, and shalt bring me up again from the depths of the earth.

This is a prophecy speaking of the Resurrection of the Lord Jesus Christ. Always remember, because He lives, we shall live also. He paid the price for us, now let us live for Him.

(Read Psalm 34:22)

*****

NOVEMBER 4

2 Timothy 1:12 (KJV) For the which cause I also suffer these things: nevertheless I am not ashamed: for I know whom I have believed, and am persuaded that he is able to keep that which I have committed unto him against that day.

Paul is not ashamed of the things he had to go through because of his ministry for Jesus Christ. We should not be ashamed of our work for the Lord either. Paul believed in the Lord, and he knew the Lord was able to keep him and protect him from everything. He also knew that Jesus was able to take care of him even until the Rapture.

(Read 2 Timothy 4:8)

*****

NOVEMBER 5

Philippians 1:6 (KJV) Being confident of this very thing, that he which hath begun a good work in you will perform *it* until the day of Jesus Christ:

When we were saved by Grace, through Faith, Jesus began a work in us. Not only is He able to begin the work, but He continues the work in us also. He has promised to keep us now and forever.

(Read Psalm 138:8)

NOVEMBER 6

Psalms 72:17 (KJV) His name shall endure for ever: his name shall be continued as long as the sun: and *men* shall be blessed in him: all nations shall call him blessed.

The name of Jesus shall stand forever. All nations shall be blessed because of Him. This rules out Muhammad, Buddha, and all others. All men everywhere shall call Jesus blessed.

(Read Psalm 106:48)

*****

NOVEMBER 7

2 Timothy 4:6-7 (KJV) (6) For I am now ready to be offered, and the time of my departure is at hand. (7) I have fought a good fight, I have finished *my* course, I have kept the faith:

Paul knew the time for leaving this world was near. He was ready to go. He was ready to meet Jesus. He felt he had fought a good fight, and he had not let the Lord down. He had finished all the work the Lord had given him to do. Most of all, Paul had kept the faith. When it comes time for us to leave this world, will we be able to give a similar testimony?

(Read Acts 20:24)

*****

NOVEMBER 8

Romans 16:20 (KJV) And the God of peace shall bruise Satan under your feet shortly. The grace of our Lord Jesus Christ *be* with you. Amen.

God has promised, if we trust Jesus and what He did on Calvary, that He will provide victory over all Satan tries to do against us. Paul goes ahead and gives his standard benediction that he uses in his letters. Let us not forget God's promise, and stand firm on it.

(Read 2 Corinthians 13:14)

*****

NOVEMBER 9

Romans 7:24-25 (KJV) (24) O wretched man that I am! who shall deliver me from the body of this death? (25) I thank God through Jesus Christ our Lord. So then with the mind I myself serve the law of God; but with the flesh the law of sin.

If we try to live for God in our own strength and abilities, and not by faith, then we are wretched and miserable. Living for God can only be done through faith in Jesus and Him crucified. Paul goes on to tell us, deliverance comes only through faith in Jesus and His death on Calvary. When we try to serve God through our own efforts, then we allow the sin nature to take control, and we have religion instead of salvation, in effect, walking away from God.

(Read 1 Corinthians 15:57)

*****

NOVEMBER 10

Psalms 49:15 (KJV) But God will redeem my soul from the power of the grave: for he shall receive me. *Selah*

This is referring to the resurrection, which takes place at the Rapture of the Church. What a glorious day that will be, when we lay down mortality, and take on immortality.

(Read Psalm 73:24)

*****

NOVEMBER 11

Job 16:22 (KJV) When a few years are come, then I shall go the way *whence* I shall not return.

Job knows how short human life is. In fact, he believes his life is almost over. We as Christians need to realize we have no promise of what tomorrow will bring. Today may be the day the Lord comes for us, or maybe tomorrow. We need to make sure our lives are ready for the Lord to come back today.

(Read Matthew 24:36)

*****

NOVEMBER 12

Psalms 23:4 (KJV) Yea, though I walk through the valley of the shadow of death, I will fear no evil: for thou *art* with me; thy rod and thy staff they comfort me.

Even though Satan can mount some terrible attacks on us, we do not have to fear them. We are to allow the Good Shepherd to fight for us. The only fight the Bible tells us to fight is the "Good Fight of Faith". The rod and staff of Jesus is constantly fighting back the powers of darkness for our benefit.

(Read Psalm 138:7)

*****

NOVEMBER 13

2 Peter 3:10 (KJV) But the day of the Lord will come as a thief in the night; in the which the heavens shall pass away with a great noise, and the elements shall melt with fervent heat, the earth also and the works that are therein shall be burned up.

At the conclusion of the Millennium, the Day of the Lord shall come very unexpectedly. At that time all the elements will melt, and then God will reform the new earth. He will by preparing for our eternity. Are you prepared for eternity?

(Read 2 Peter 3:12-13)

*****

NOVEMBER 14

Job 19:25-26 (KJV) (25) For I know *that* my redeemer liveth, and *that* he shall stand at the latter *day* upon the earth: (26) And *though* after my skin *worms* destroy this *body*, yet in my flesh shall I see God:

Job understood the concept of the Lord Jesus Christ, even though he did not understand the details. Job knew his redeemer was coming, and knew he was living for Him. Job also knew that one day he would stand before his Redeemer. One day we too shall stand before our redeemer. Are you ready to do that?

(Read 1 John 3:2)

*****

NOVEMBER 15

Revelation 1:7 (KJV) Behold, he cometh with clouds; and every eye shall see him, and they *also* which pierced him: and all kindreds of the earth shall wail because of him. Even so, Amen.

The main theme of the Book of Revelation, is the Second Coming of Jesus Christ. The word "cloud" in this verse is referring to great numbers of saints. When Jesus sets foot on the Mount of Olives, billions of people will see Him. At that time, even the Jews will know Jesus is their Messiah. The "wailing" spoken of here, is because of the Judgment Jesus will bring upon the world for all its sin. It is up to us to make sure we are ready for the Lord when He comes in the Rapture.

(Read Revelation 21:6)

*****

NOVEMBER 16

2 Corinthians 5:10 (KJV) For we must all appear before the judgment seat of Christ; that every one may receive the things *done* in *his* body, according to that he hath done, whether *it be* good or bad.

The Judgment seat of Christ will take place in Heaven. It will probably be immediately before the Second Coming of Jesus Christ. This judgment has to do with the life we lived for the Lord. Sins will not be judged here. What will be judged, is our motivation and faithfulness while living for the Lord. It is time now to exam ourselves concerning our hearts and motives.

(Read Romans 14:10)

*****

NOVEMBER 17

Romans 8:33-34 (KJV) (33) Who shall lay any thing to the charge of God's elect? *It is* God that justifieth. (34) Who *is* he that condemneth? *It is* Christ that died, yea rather, that is risen again, who is even at the right hand of God,

who also maketh intercession for us.

Paul is asking a major question here. What he is asking is "Who shall pronounce those guilty whom God has pronounced righteous?" We need to remember, it is God who sets the rules for justification. It has nothing to do with man. Man has no right, or authority to condemn God's Justification Plan. If a person condemns a believer who is trusting the Lord for Justification, they are at the same time condemning Jesus Christ. Let's keep our eyes on Jesus, and not on man.

(Read Hebrews 7:25)

*****

NOVEMBER 18

1 Corinthians 6:2 (KJV) Do ye not know that the saints shall judge the world? and if the world shall be judged by you, are ye unworthy to judge the smallest matters?

This verse is referring to the Millennial and Eternal Reins of Jesus Christ and His saints. If we serve the Lord with our whole heart right now, there is coming a day when we will rule and reign with Jesus Christ. What a day that will be.

(Read Daniel 7:22)

*****

NOVEMBER 19

Jude 1:24 (KJV) Now unto him that is able to keep you from falling, and to present *you* faultless before the presence of his glory with exceeding joy,

The one who is able to keep us falling is the Lord Jesus Christ. This was all brought about by His sacrifice on Calvary. Because of Jesus, we will one day stand blameless before the Judgment seat. At that time, the Holy Ghost will present us to the Father "with exceeding joy".

(Read Ephesians 1:4)

*****

NOVEMBER 20

1 Corinthians 15:54 (KJV) So when this corruptible shall have put on incorruption, and this mortal shall have put on immortality, then shall be brought to pass the saying that is written, Death is swallowed up in victory.

There is coming a day when we shall lay aside the sin nature we are constantly fighting with. When that happens, we will put on the Divine Nature, which is totally controlled by the Holy Ghost. At that time this mortal body which is subject to death, shall put on immortality, which will never die. Then shall we receive all of the benefits Jesus provided for us at Calvary.

(Read 1 Corinthians 15:42-44)

NOVEMBER 21

Philippians 3:21 (KJV) Who shall change our vile body, that it may be fashioned like unto his glorious body, according to the working whereby he is able even to subdue all things unto himself.

At the Resurrection, the Lord Jesus will change our mortal body. It is then that every Saint of God will receive a Glorified body. All this is provided by the price Jesus paid at Calvary. Then shall we ever be with the Lord.

(Read 1 Corinthians 15:51)

*****

NOVEMBER 22

Philippians 1:21-23 (KJV) (21) For to me to live *is* Christ, and to die *is* gain. (22) But if I live in the flesh, this *is* the fruit of my labour: yet what I shall choose I wot not. (23) For I am in a strait betwixt two, having a desire to depart, and to be with Christ; which is far better:

Paul's only desire was to preach Jesus and Him crucified. The longer he lived, the longer he could live for, and preach Jesus Christ. He is saying, if he died, that it would be personal gain, but not for the work of God. Souls being saved, and lives being changed by the message of the sacrifice of Jesus, was the fruit of his labor. Paul went on to say, if he had to make a choice, he is not sure which he would choose. Paul is sharing with us a personal glimpse into his life, showing us where our hearts should be.

(Read 2 Corinthians 5:8)

*****

NOVEMBER 23

1 Thessalonians 4:17 (KJV) Then we which are alive *and* remain shall be caught up together with them in the clouds, to meet the Lord in the air: and so shall we ever be with the Lord.

If we are alive at the time of the Rapture, we shall be caught up with the resurrected dead. The word "clouds" is referring to clouds, or a large number of saints, and not regular clouds. Then, we will meet the Lord in the air. At that time, the Lord will not come to the earth. This will be the greatest gathering of believers in the history of the church.

(Read 1 Corinthians 15:52-53)

*****

NOVEMBER 24

2 Timothy 2:11-12 (KJV) (11) *It is* a faithful saying: For if we be dead with *him*, we shall also live with *him*: (12) If we suffer, we shall also reign with *him*: if we deny *him*, he also will deny us:

Jesus died as our substitute on the cross. Our faith in what He did, places us there on the cross with Him. Since we are dead with Him, we will live in Eternity with Him. This will happen when we receive our resurrection body. We were planted together with Jesus in death, and it was all done at the Cross of Calvary.

(Read 1 Timothy 1:15)

*****

NOVEMBER 25

1 John 3:2 (KJV) Beloved, now are we the sons of God, and it doth not yet appear what we shall be: but we know that, when he shall appear, we shall be like him; for we shall see him as he is.

We are the sons of God because of what Jesus did for us at Calvary. John says in this verse, that when we are resurrected, we do not know what our new glorified body will be like. He goes on to say, when Jesus appears at the rapture, this body will change, and our glorified body will be like the body of Jesus. Won't that be wonderful?

(Read John 17:24)

*****

NOVEMBER 26

2 Corinthians 5:1 (KJV) For we know that if our earthly house of *this* tabernacle were dissolved, we have a building of God, an house not made with hands, eternal in the heavens.

What a promise! When we lose this physical body, which by the way is not permanent, God has prepared a glorified one for us. We will receive this new glorified body at the resurrection. This glorified body which is not made with hands, is created by God, and it will live and last forever.

(Read Romans 8:23)

*****

NOVEMBER 27

1 Corinthians 13:12 (KJV) For now we see through a glass, darkly; but then face to face: now I know in part; but then shall I know even as also I am known.

Right now, before the resurrection, we do not see things clearly. You might say, we see these spiritual things in a very dim light. But, once the resurrection takes place, we shall see everything clearly and openly. Right now, we have just a little bit of knowledge, but then, everything will be revealed to us.

(Read 2 Corinthians 3:18)

*****

NOVEMBER 28

2 Timothy 4:8 (KJV) Henceforth there is laid up for me a crown of righteousness, which the Lord, the righteous judge, shall give me at that day: and not to me only, but unto all them also that love his appearing.

As children of God, a Crown of Righteousness has been prepared for us. This crown shall be presented at the Judgment seat of Christ, to everyone who has overcome this world. You must be watching for Him when He comes. Are you watching?

(Read 1 Corinthians 9:25)

*****

NOVEMBER 29

1 Thessalonians 2:19 (KJV) For what *is* our hope, or joy, or crown of rejoicing? *Are* not even ye in the presence of our Lord Jesus Christ at his coming?

We face many annoyances now, but the Apostle Paul is showing us past the things of this world, where Satan will no longer be able to hinder us. He is pointing us to the Rapture of the Church, which will remove us from this present world.

(Read 2 Peter 1:16)

*****

NOVEMBER 30

2 Peter 3:14 (KJV) Wherefore, beloved, seeing that ye look for such things, be diligent that ye may be found of him in peace, without spot, and blameless.

If we believe the Bible is true, then we believe what it has to say about future Prophetic events. We must keep our faith in Jesus Christ and Him crucified. Doing so will guarantee that we are ready for End-time events.

(Read 1 Thessalonians 2:19)

*****

CHAPTER 12 - DECEMBER

DECEMBER 1

Romans 6:22-23 (KJV) (22) But now being made free from sin, and become servants to God, ye have your fruit unto holiness, and the end everlasting life. (23) For the wages of sin *is* death; but the gift of God *is* eternal life through Jesus Christ our Lord.

Since coming to Jesus Christ, we have been set free from our sin nature. We have actually become slaves of God. As long as we continue to have faith in Jesus and Him crucified, the Holy Ghost will bring about the fruit of holiness in our lives, and in the end, eternal life. We have the choice of receiving life through Jesus Christ, or eternal death by not keeping our faith in Jesus and what He did on Calvary. The wages of sin is spiritual death, which is eternal torment, but God's gift is eternal life through Jesus.

(Read Romans 5:12)

DECEMBER 2

Hebrews 9:12 (KJV) Neither by the blood of goats and calves, but by his own blood he entered in once into the holy place, having obtained eternal redemption *for us*.

Paul explains here, that the blood of bulls and goats could not forgive sin. That is why sacrifices were made on a regular basis. But, the price for all sin was paid by the **blood** of Jesus. Jesus did what no other priest was ever able to do. He offered a complete sacrifice, which means it never had to be repeated again. The offering that Jesus made on the cross provided Eternal Redemption for us.

(Read Hebrews 10:19)

*****

DECEMBER 3

Ephesians 1:13-14 (KJV) (13) In whom ye also *trusted*, after that ye heard the word of truth, the gospel of your salvation: in whom also after that ye believed, ye were sealed with that holy Spirit of promise, (14) Which is the earnest of our inheritance until the redemption of the purchased possession, unto the praise of his glory.

You trusted in Jesus after you heard the Word of Truth. That Word of Truth is the message of Jesus and His crucifixion. Also, when you believed, you were sealed with the Holy Ghost. This is the down payment of our promise. This guarantees that we will receive our complete inheritance at the Resurrection. It was totally purchased by the **blood** of Jesus, and will be completely fulfilled at the Resurrection.

(Read Romans 8:23)

*****

DECEMBER 4

2 Corinthians 5:6-8 (KJV) (6) Therefore *we are* always confident, knowing that, whilst we are at home in the body, we are absent from the Lord: (7) (For we walk by faith, not by sight:) (8) We are confident, *I say*, and willing rather to be absent from the body, and to be present with the Lord.

Paul is making an important distinction between a person and his physical body. He said while we are at home in this body, we are absent from the Lord. Life is a journey we walk by faith, for we are actually pilgrims in this world we live in. But, he went on to say, that when we are absent from this body, we are then present with the Lord.

(Read 1 Corinthians 2:9–10)

*****

DECEMBER 5

Hebrews 4:9 (KJV) There remaineth therefore a rest to the people of God.

Think about this. The Law could not provide a rest for God's people. But, what the Law could not do, Jesus Christ did. This rest is only found by putting our faith in Jesus and His crucifixion.

(Read Hebrews 3:12)

*****

DECEMBER 6

Revelation 19:9 (KJV) And he saith unto me, Write, Blessed *are* they which are called unto the marriage supper of the Lamb. And he saith unto me, These are the true sayings of God.

We will be invited to the Marriage Supper of the Lamb, because Jesus made all of this possible by His death on the cross of Calvary. He is the Lamb of God, the perfect sacrifice who died in our place, and then was resurrected from the dead.

(Read Revelation 21:5)

*****

DECEMBER 7

Hebrews 9:15 (KJV) And for this cause he is the mediator of the new testament, that by means of death, for the redemption of the transgressions *that were* under the first testament, they which are called might receive the promise of eternal inheritance.

Jesus is the mediator of the New Covenant. By His death on the cross, He atoned for all sin. This was necessary in order for man to be saved. The death of Christ was for those before Christ, just as much as for those after the Lord left this earth. The sacrifice of Jesus guarantees the redemption of everyone who dies in the Faith. Let us remember that the blood of bulls and goats could not redeem man, but the ***blood*** of Jesus does.

(Read Acts 20:32)

*****

DECEMBER 8

Luke 22:29-30 (KJV) (29) And I appoint unto you a kingdom, as my Father hath appointed unto me; (30) That ye may eat and drink at my table in my kingdom, and sit on thrones judging the twelve tribes of Israel.

As children of God, He has made us joint heirs with Jesus Christ. He goes on to talk about the coming Kingdom Age, and the Disciples sitting on thrones, judging the twelve Tribes of Israel. Only the twelve Apostles will be able to enjoy this. But, as we have already discussed, Jesus will make us kings and priests in His Kingdom.

(Read 2 Timothy 2:12)

*****

DECEMBER 9

John 14:2 (KJV) In my Father's house are many mansions: if *it were* not *so*, I would have told you. I go to prepare a place for you.

This verse describes Heaven as being a very large place. It is larger even than anything we can ever imagine or comprehend. There is no doubt that Jesus is even speaking from personal knowledge of everything He was talking about. Jesus even refers to the fact that He will be personally overseeing all the work that is being done just for us.

(Read John 12:26)

*****

DECEMBER 10

Luke 23:43 (KJV) And Jesus said unto him, Verily I say unto thee, To day shalt thou be with me in paradise.

This is a statement of fact that Jesus made to the thief on the cross. That very day, the thief was with Jesus in Paradise. Then, three days later, He took all the Old Testament saints to Heaven. What He did for the Old Testament saints at that time, He will be doing for us in the near future.

(Read Romans 6:5)

*****

DECEMBER 11

Revelation 21:27 (KJV) And there shall in no wise enter into it any thing that defileth, neither *whatsoever* worketh abomination, or *maketh* a lie: but they which are written in the Lamb's book of life.

Not everyone can enter into Heaven, for all sin has been forever banished. Only those who have been saved by putting their faith in Jesus and His crucifixion have their names in the Lamb's Book of Life. Only those whose name is in the Lambs Book of Life are allowed to enter into Heaven.

(Read Revelation 3:5)

*****

DECEMBER 12

Psalms 16:11 (KJV) Thou wilt show me the path of life: in thy presence *is* fulness of joy; at thy right hand *there are* pleasures for evermore.

The path of life David is referring to here, is Eternal Life. Being able to enter Heaven and meet the promised Messiah brings complete and total joy. Finally, Eternal Life with the one who made intercession for us all, by His death on Calvary.

(Read Psalm 17:15)

*****

DECEMBER 13

Revelation 7:15 (KJV) Therefore are they before the throne of God, and serve him day and night in his temple: and he that sitteth on the throne shall dwell among them.

The group spoken of here, came out of the Great Tribulation. The presence of God will forever be with all of the saints of God.

(Read Isaiah 49:10)

*****

DECEMBER 14

Revelation 21:4 (KJV) And God shall wipe away all tears from their eyes; and there shall be no more death, neither sorrow, nor crying, neither shall there be any more pain: for the former things are passed away.

This is a beautiful passage. The original Greek actually says that God will wipe away "every teardrop". None of the results of sin will be in Heaven. All of the effects of the fall of man will be totally gone.

(Read Revelation 7:17)

*****

DECEMBER 15

Revelation 22:3 (KJV) And there shall be no more curse: but the throne of God and of the Lamb shall be in it; and his servants shall serve him:

By the use of the word "lamb" here, we are told all of this is made possible because of Jesus and His sacrifice on Calvary. Every believer here will love the Lord so much, they will be more than happy to serve Him for eternity.

(Read 1 Corinthians 13:12)

*****

DECEMBER 16

Revelation 22:5 (KJV) And there shall be no night there; and they need no candle, neither light of the sun; for the Lord God giveth them light: and they shall reign for ever and ever.

This verse is speaking of the New Jerusalem. Jesus will be the source of light for this beautiful city. The servants of God will rule here as kings for eternity.

(Read 1 Peter 2:9)

DECEMBER 17

Luke 20:35-36 (KJV) (35) But they which shall be accounted worthy to obtain that world, and the resurrection from the dead, neither marry, nor are given in marriage: (36) Neither can they die any more: for they are equal unto the angels; and are the children of God, being the children of the resurrection.

Only those who have been Born Again will be able to enter into this world. This verse states emphatically that there is a Resurrection. At this time, all saints of God will have glorified bodies, and there will be no more death. Being equal to the angels is speaking of immortality. Born again believers will be called "the Children of the Resurrection", simply because of the Born Again experience.

(Read Romans 8:23)

*****

DECEMBER 18

Revelation 5:9 (KJV) And they sung a new song, saying, Thou art worthy to take the book, and to open the seals thereof: for thou wast slain, and hast redeemed us to God by thy blood out of every kindred, and tongue, and people, and nation;

It is those who are redeemed, who will be singing. The song proclaims that by the death of Jesus, He is able to do what no one else can do. The fact that He was slain on the cross has made everything possible. This is how redemption has been purchased. This verse also proclaims the fact that salvation purchased by the death of Jesus applies to all classes of people on the earth.

(Read 1 Corinthians 6:20)

*****

DECEMBER 19

Revelation 7:14-15 (KJV) (14) And I said unto him, Sir, thou knowest. And he said to me, These are they which came out of great tribulation, and have washed their robes, and made them white in the blood of the Lamb. (15) Therefore are they before the throne of God, and serve him day and night in his temple: and he that sitteth on the throne shall dwell among them.

This verse is speaking about a specific group of people. They had gotten saved during the Great Tribulation, and they trusted Jesus and His sacrifice on Calvary, even up to and including being martyred. They are shown here standing before the Throne of God, serving God twenty-four hours a day. It finally says that God will dwell among them. He will dwell among us also.

(Read Isaiah 1:18)

*****

DECEMBER 20

Revelation 21:3 (KJV) And I heard a great voice out of heaven saying, Behold, the tabernacle of God *is* with men, and he will dwell with them, and they shall be his people, and God himself shall be with them, *and be* their God.

According to the best manuscripts, the "Voice" being heard was coming "out of the Throne". That "Voice" is proclaiming what God has intended from the very beginning. The Tabernacle of God is with men. God will dwell with His people. They shall be called His people. God will be their God. If we are saved, we will be counted in this number.

(Read Revelation 22:3)

*****

DECEMBER 21

John 17:24 (KJV) Father, I will that they also, whom thou hast given me, be with me where I am; that they may behold my glory, which thou hast given me: for thou lovedst me before the foundation of the world.

Jesus lets us know here that He is one with the Father. Jesus goes on to talk about the Exaltation that He will receive in just a few hours, when He is resurrected. Finally, He proclaims His pre-existence with the father, which states His Deity.

(Read Ephesians 1:4)

*****

DECEMBER 22

Revelation 21:7 (KJV) He that overcometh shall inherit all things; and I will be his God, and he shall be my son.

The only way to be an over-comer, is to place your faith in Jesus and His crucifixion. In doing so, the Holy Ghost can work in your life to bring about the Fruit of the Spirit. The over-comer is also adopted into the family of God, where God makes him a joint heir with Jesus Christ.

(Read 2 Corinthians 6:18)

*****

DECEMBER 23

Hebrews 12:22-23 (KJV) (22) But ye are come unto mount Sion, and unto the city of the living God, the heavenly Jerusalem, and to an innumerable company of angels, (23) To the general assembly and church of the firstborn, which are written in heaven, and to God the Judge of all, and to the spirits of just men made perfect,

It is impossible to reach this city by Law, it must be reached through Grace. There will be a company of angels there, and it will be so large, that it cannot be counted. From the time of Abel, all the way through the Second Coming, the price of

Redemption has been the **blood** of Jesus. Because of the **blood**, God has already judged the "Church of the Firstborn", and declared everyone justified in His sight. Thank God for Justification by Faith.

(Read Philippians 3:20-21)

*****

DECEMBER 24

Matthew 13:43 (KJV) Then shall the righteous shine forth as the sun in the kingdom of their Father. Who hath ears to hear, let him hear.

This verse is referring to the coming Kingdom Age. In this perfect age that is yet to come, we will shine forth as children of the Father. We are to have complete assurance about this promise from God.

(Read Matthew 26:29)

*****

DECEMBER 25

Revelation 7:9 (KJV) After this I beheld, and, lo, a great multitude, which no man could number, of all nations, and kindreds, and people, and tongues, stood before the throne, and before the Lamb, clothed with white robes, and palms in their hands;

This is those martyrs who gave their lives for the Lord during the Great Tribulation. It is a crowd of people so large, that they could not be counted, and they are all saved during the Great Tribulation. We know, that since the word "Lamb" is used here, that they too have been washed in the **blood** of the Lamb. We see them standing there in wedding garments that are purest white. God has just as much in store for us.

(Read Revelation 5:13)

*****

DECEMBER 26

Revelation 5:10 (KJV) And hast made us unto our God kings and priests: and we shall reign on the earth.

As we are His children, redeemed by His **blood**, Jesus will make us kings and priests with Him. All this will be taking place during the Millennial Reign of Jesus Christ upon the earth.

(Read Revelation 1:6)

*****

DECEMBER 27

Psalms 31:19 (KJV) *Oh* how great *is* thy goodness, which thou hast laid up for them that fear thee; *which* thou hast wrought for them that trust in thee before the sons of men!

God is so good, and serving the Lord will bring great blessings, even Eternal Life. On the other hand, failing to serve God will bring great judgment, which is eternal torment.

(Read. 1 Corinthians 2:9)

*****

DECEMBER 28

Revelation 7:17 (KJV) For the Lamb which is in the midst of the throne shall feed them, and shall lead them unto living fountains of waters: and God shall wipe away all tears from their eyes.

Not only did the Lamb save them, but He will also "feed them". Our Salvation comes because of what Jesus did at the cross. Now, since we are saved we now "live" because of what Jesus did at the cross. The "Living Waters" are symbolic of the Holy Ghost. Lastly, God shall wipe away each tear, from each eye, for everything that causes sorrow will be gone forever.

(Read Isaiah 25:8)

*****

DECEMBER 29

Psalms 17:15 (KJV) As for me, I will behold thy face in righteousness: I shall be satisfied, when I awake, with thy likeness.

What joy shall overtake us, when we see Jesus face to face. At that time, we will be totally satisfied, especially when we see we are in His likeness.

(Read Job 33:26)

*****

DECEMBER 30

Revelation 3:12 (KJV) Him that overcometh will I make a pillar in the temple of my God, and he shall go no more out: and I will write upon him the name of my God, and the name of the city of my God, *which is* new Jerusalem, which cometh down out of heaven from my God: and *I will write upon him* my new name.

The "over-comer" is someone who trusts completely in Jesus Christ, and what He did on Calvary. At the time this verse is speaking about, we will be constantly in the presence of God. Jesus at that time see that we are totally and completely identified with Him. Jesus is the source of all things now and forever, because of what He did at Calvary.

(Read Revelation 3:5)

*****

DECEMBER 31

Daniel 12:12-13 (KJV) (12) Blessed *is* he that waiteth, and cometh to the thousand three hundred and five and thirty days. (13) But go thou thy way till the end *be*: for thou shalt rest, and stand in thy lot at the end of the days.

Those who come to this time will be blessed. These verses are talking about the beginning of the Kingdom Age, and about the events that will come about to establish the beginning of the Kingdom. Daniel is told here that he will die, and become a part of the First Resurrection. The Lord told him until that time he must rest. Daniel will have a part in the things that will take place after the Second Coming. What a celebration we will all be taking part in!

(Read Daniel 12:9-10)

*****

If You Would Like To Be Saved,

Pray This Prayer With Your Whole Heart

Dear Heavenly Father, I realize that have broken your laws and I am a sinner. I understand that my sin has separated me from you. I am sorry and I ask you to forgive me. I accept the fact that your son Jesus Christ died for me, was resurrected, and is alive today and hears my prayers. I now open my heart and invite Jesus in to become my Lord and Saviour. I give Him control and ask that He would rule and reign in my heart so that His perfect will would be accomplished in my life. In Jesus name I pray. Amen.

Congratulations!

If you prayed this prayer in all sincerity, you are now a Child of God. But, there are a few things that you need to do to follow up on your commitment to the Lord.

(1) **Get baptized (full immersion) in water as commanded by Jesus**
(2) **Tell someone else about your new faith in Jesus.**
(3) **Spend time with God each day through prayer and Bible reading**
(4) **Seek fellowship with other followers of Jesus**

So that we might rejoice with you, we invite you to contact us and let us know about the decision you made!

You may contact Rev. Smith at: **devotions1day@gmail.com**

Made in the USA
Las Vegas, NV
25 November 2023

81460329R00116